Carnegie Commission on Higher Education
Sponsored Research Studies

MODELS AND MAVERICKS:
A PROFILE OF PRIVATE LIBERAL ARTS
COLLEGES
Morris T. Keeton

BETWEEN TWO WORLDS:
A PROFILE OF NEGRO HIGHER EDUCATION
Frank Bowles and Frank A. DeCosta

BREAKING THE ACCESS BARRIERS:
A PROFILE OF TWO-YEAR COLLEGES
Leland L. Medsker and Dale Tillery

ANY PERSON, ANY STUDY:
AN ESSAY ON HIGHER EDUCATION IN THE
UNITED STATES
Eric Ashby

THE NEW DEPRESSION IN HIGHER
EDUCATION:
A STUDY OF FINANCIAL CONDITIONS AT 41
COLLEGES AND UNIVERSITIES
Earl F. Cheit

FINANCING MEDICAL EDUCATION:
AN ANALYSIS OF ALTERNATIVE POLICIES
AND MECHANISMS
Rashi Fein and Gerald I. Weber

HIGHER EDUCATION IN NINE COUNTRIES:
A COMPARATIVE STUDY OF COLLEGES AND
UNIVERSITIES ABROAD
*Barbara B. Burn, Philip G. Altbach, Clark Kerr,
and James A. Perkins*

BRIDGES TO UNDERSTANDING:
INTERNATIONAL PROGRAMS OF AMERICAN
COLLEGES AND UNIVERSITIES
Irwin T. Sanders and Jennifer C. Ward

GRADUATE AND PROFESSIONAL EDUCATION,
1980:
A SURVEY OF INSTITUTIONAL PLANS
Lewis B. Mayhew

THE AMERICAN COLLEGE AND AMERICAN
CULTURE:
SOCIALIZATION AS A FUNCTION OF HIGHER
EDUCATION
Oscar Handlin and Mary F. Handlin

RECENT ALUMNI AND HIGHER EDUCATION:
A SURVEY OF COLLEGE GRADUATES
Joe L. Spaeth and Andrew M. Greeley

CHANGE IN EDUCATIONAL POLICY:
SELF-STUDIES IN SELECTED COLLEGES AND
UNIVERSITIES
Dwight R. Ladd

STATE OFFICIALS AND HIGHER EDUCATION:
A SURVEY OF THE OPINIONS AND
EXPECTATIONS OF POLICY MAKERS IN NINE
STATES
Heinz Eulau and Harold Quinley

ACADEMIC DEGREE STRUCTURES:
INNOVATIVE APPROACHES
PRINCIPLES OF REFORM IN DEGREE
STRUCTURES IN THE UNITED STATES
Stephen H. Spurr

COLLEGES OF THE FORGOTTEN AMERICANS:
A PROFILE OF STATE COLLEGES AND
REGIONAL UNIVERSITIES
E. Alden Dunham

FROM BACKWATER TO MAINSTREAM:
A PROFILE OF CATHOLIC HIGHER
EDUCATION
Andrew M. Greeley

THE ECONOMICS OF THE MAJOR PRIVATE
UNIVERSITIES
William G. Bowen
(Out of print, but available from University Microfilms.)

THE FINANCE OF HIGHER EDUCATION
Howard R. Bowen
(Out of print, but available from University Microfilms.)

ALTERNATIVE METHODS OF FEDERAL
FUNDING FOR HIGHER EDUCATION
Ron Wolk
(Out of print, but available from University Microfilms.)

INVENTORY OF CURRENT RESEARCH ON
HIGHER EDUCATION 1968
Dale M. Heckman and Warren Bryan Martin
(Out of print, but available from University Microfilms.)

The following technical reports are available from the Carnegie Commission on Higher Education, 1947 Center Street, Berkeley, California 94704.

RESOURCE USE IN HIGHER EDUCATION:
TRENDS IN OUTPUT AND INPUTS, 1930–1967
June O'Neill

TRENDS AND PROJECTIONS OF PHYSICIANS
IN THE UNITED STATES 1967–2002
Mark S. Blumberg

MAY 1970:
THE CAMPUS AFTERMATH OF CAMBODIA
AND KENT STATE
Richard E. Peterson and John A. Bilorusky

MENTAL ABILITY AND HIGHER EDUCATIONAL
ATTAINMENT IN THE 20TH CENTURY
Paul Taubman and Terence Wales

AMERICAN COLLEGE AND UNIVERSITY
ENROLLMENT TRENDS IN 1971
Richard E. Peterson

PAPERS ON EFFICIENCY IN THE
MANAGEMENT OF HIGHER EDUCATION
*Alexander M. Mood, Colin Bell,
Lawrence Bogard, Helen Brownlee,
and Joseph McCloskey*

AN INVENTORY OF ACADEMIC INNOVATION
AND REFORM
Ann Heiss

ESTIMATING THE RETURNS TO EDUCATION:
A DISAGGREGATED APPROACH
Richard S. Eckaus

SOURCES OF FUNDS TO COLLEGES AND
UNIVERSITIES
June O'Neill

NEW DEPRESSION IN HIGHER
EDUCATION—TWO YEARS LATER
Earl F. Cheit

The following reprints are available from the Carnegie Commission on Higher Education, 1947 Center Street, Berkeley, California 94704.

ACCELERATED PROGRAMS OF MEDICAL EDUCATION, *by Mark S. Blumberg, reprinted from* JOURNAL OF MEDICAL EDUCATION, *vol. 46, no. 8, August 1971.**

SCIENTIFIC MANPOWER FOR 1970–1985, *by Allan M. Cartter, reprinted from* SCIENCE, *vol. 172, no. 3979, pp. 132–140, April 9, 1971.*

A NEW METHOD OF MEASURING STATES' HIGHER EDUCATION BURDEN, *by Neil Timm, reprinted from* THE JOURNAL OF HIGHER EDUCATION, *vol. 42, no. 1, pp. 27–33, January 1971.**

REGENT WATCHING, *by Earl F. Cheit, reprinted from* AGB REPORTS, *vol. 13, no. 6, pp. 4–13, March 1971.*

COLLEGE GENERATIONS—FROM THE 1930s TO THE 1960s *by Seymour M. Lipset and Everett C. Ladd, Jr., reprinted from* THE PUBLIC INTEREST, *no. 25, Summer 1971.*

AMERICAN SOCIAL SCIENTISTS AND THE GROWTH OF CAMPUS POLITICAL ACTIVISM IN THE 1960s, *by Everett C. Ladd, Jr., and Seymour M. Lipset, reprinted from* SOCIAL SCIENCES INFORMATION, *vol. 10, no. 2, April 1971.*

THE POLITICS OF AMERICAN POLITICAL SCIENTISTS, *by Everett C. Ladd, Jr., and Seymour M. Lipset, reprinted from* PS, *vol. 4, no. 2, Spring 1971.**

THE DIVIDED PROFESSORIATE, *by Seymour M. Lipset and Everett C. Ladd, Jr., reprinted from* CHANGE, *vol. 3, no. 3, pp. 54–60, May 1971.**

JEWISH ACADEMICS IN THE UNITED STATES: THEIR ACHIEVEMENTS, CULTURE AND POLITICS, *by Seymour M. Lipset and Everett C. Ladd, Jr., reprinted from* AMERICAN JEWISH YEAR BOOK, *1971.*

THE UNHOLY ALLIANCE AGAINST THE CAMPUS, *by Kenneth Keniston and Michael Lerner, reprinted from NEW YORK TIMES MAGAZINE, November 8, 1970.*

PRECARIOUS PROFESSORS: NEW PATTERNS OF REPRESENTATION, by Joseph W. Garbarino, reprinted from INDUSTRIAL RELATIONS, vol. 10, no. 1, February 1971.*

. . . AND WHAT PROFESSORS THINK: ABOUT STUDENT PROTEST AND MANNERS, MORALS, POLITICS, AND CHAOS ON THE CAMPUS, by Seymour Martin Lipset and Everett C. Ladd, Jr., reprinted from PSYCHOLOGY TODAY, November 1970.*

DEMAND AND SUPPLY IN U.S. HIGHER EDUCATION: A PROGRESS REPORT, by Roy Radner and Leonard S. Miller, reprinted from AMERICAN ECONOMIC REVIEW, May 1970.*

RESOURCES FOR HIGHER EDUCATION: AN ECONOMIST'S VIEW, by Theodore W. Schultz, reprinted from JOURNAL OF POLITICAL ECONOMY, vol. 76, no. 3, University of Chicago, May/June 1968.*

INDUSTRIAL RELATIONS AND UNIVERSITY RELATIONS, by Clark Kerr, reprinted from PROCEEDINGS OF THE 21ST ANNUAL WINTER MEETING OF THE INDUSTRIAL RELATIONS RESEARCH ASSOCIATION, pp. 15–25.*

NEW CHALLENGES TO THE COLLEGE AND UNIVERSITY, by Clark Kerr, reprinted from Kermit Gordon (ed.), AGENDA FOR THE NATION, The Brookings Institution, Washington, D.C., 1968.*

PRESIDENTIAL DISCONTENT, by Clark Kerr, reprinted from David C. Nichols (ed.), PERSPECTIVES ON CAMPUS TENSIONS: PAPERS PREPARED FOR THE SPECIAL COMMITTEE ON CAMPUS TENSIONS, American Council on Education, Washington, D.C., September 1970.*

STUDENT PROTEST—AN INSTITUTIONAL AND NATIONAL PROFILE, by Harold Hodgkinson, reprinted from THE RECORD, vol. 71, no. 4, May 1970.*

WHAT'S BUGGING THE STUDENTS?, by Kenneth Keniston, reprinted from EDUCATIONAL RECORD, American Council on Education, Washington, D.C., Spring 1970.*

THE POLITICS OF ACADEMIA, by Seymour Martin Lipset, reprinted from David C. Nichols (ed.), PERSPECTIVES ON CAMPUS TENSIONS: PAPERS PREPARED FOR THE SPECIAL COMMITTEE ON CAMPUS TENSIONS, American Council on Education, Washington, D.C., September 1970.*

INTERNATIONAL PROGRAMS OF U.S. COLLEGES AND UNIVERSITIES: PRIORITIES FOR THE SEVENTIES, by James A. Perkins, reprinted by permission of the International Council for Educational Development, Occasional Paper no. 1, July 1971.

FACULTY UNIONISM: FROM THEORY TO PRACTICE, by Joseph W. Garbarino, reprinted from INDUSTRIAL RELATIONS, vol. 11, no. 1, pp. 1–17, February 1972.

MORE FOR LESS: HIGHER EDUCATION'S NEW PRIORITY, by Virginia B. Smith, reprinted from UNIVERSAL HIGHER EDUCATION: COSTS AND BENEFITS, American Council on Education, Washington, D.C., 1971.

ACADEMIA AND POLITICS IN AMERICA, *by Seymour M. Lipset, reprinted from Thomas J. Nossiter (ed.)*, IMAGINATION AND PRECISION IN THE SOCIAL SCIENCES, *pp. 211–289, Faber and Faber, London, 1972.*

POLITICS OF ACADEMIC NATURAL SCIENTISTS AND ENGINEERS, *by Everett C. Ladd, Jr., and Seymour M. Lipset, reprinted from* SCIENCE, *vol. 176, no. 4039, pp. 1091–1100, June 9, 1972.*

THE INTELLECTUAL AS CRITIC AND REBEL: WITH SPECIAL REFERENCE TO THE UNITED STATES AND THE SOVIET UNION, *by Seymour M. Lipset and Richard B. Dobson, reprinted from* DAEDALUS, *vol. 101, no. 3, pp. 137–198, Summer 1972.*

COMING OF MIDDLE AGE IN HIGHER EDUCATION, *by Earl F. Cheit, address delivered to American Association of State Colleges and Universities and National Association of State Universities and Land-Grant Colleges, Nov. 13, 1972.*

THE NATURE AND ORIGINS OF THE CARNEGIE COMMISSION ON HIGHER EDUCATION, by Alan Pifer, *reprinted by permission of The Carnegie Commission for the Advancement of Teaching, speech delivered Oct. 16, 1972.*

THE DISTRIBUTION OF ACADEMIC TENURE IN AMERICAN HIGHER EDUCATION, *by Martin Trow, reprinted from* THE TENURE DEBATE, *Bardwell Smith (ed.), Jossey-Bass, San Francisco, 1972.*

THE POLITICS OF AMERICAN SOCIOLOGISTS, *by Seymour M. Lipset, and Everett C. Ladd, Jr., reprinted from* THE AMERICAN JOURNAL OF SOCIOLOGY, *vol. 78, no. 1, July 1972.*

*The Commission's stock of this reprint has been exhausted.

The Rise of
the Arts on
the American Campus

The Rise of the Arts on the American Campus

by Jack Morrison

Associate Director
Arts in Education Program
The JDR 3rd Fund

Thirteenth of a Series of Profiles Sponsored by
The Carnegie Commission on Higher Education

MCGRAW-HILL BOOK COMPANY
New York   St. Louis   San Francisco   Düsseldorf
London   Sydney   Toronto   Mexico   Panama
Johannesburg   Kuala Lumpur   Montreal
New Delhi   Rio de Janeiro   Singapore

*The Carnegie Commission on Higher Education,
1947 Center Street, Berkeley, California 94704,
has sponsored preparation of this profile as a
part of a continuing effort to obtain and present
significant information for public discussion.
The views expressed are those of the author.*

THE RISE OF THE ARTS ON THE AMERICAN CAMPUS

Library of Congress Cataloging in Publication Data

Morrison, Jack, date
The rise of the arts on the American campus.

"Thirteenth of a series of profiles sponsored by
the Carnegie Commission on Higher Education."
Bibliography: p.
1.   Universities and colleges—United States—
Curricula.   2.   The arts-study and teaching
United States.   I.   Carnegie Commission on Higher
Education.   II.   Title.

LB2361.5.M67   700'.71' 173   72-10456
ISBN 0-07-010055-1

123456789MAMM79876543

Contents

Foreword

The state of the arts in American higher education has improved considerably since Cotton Mather reported in 1723 that the scholars of Harvard College had filled their studies "with books which may truly be called *Satan's Library*," consisting of "plays, novels, empty and vicious pieces of poetry. . . ." But how have the arts fared on American campuses in the 250 years since Mather's report? This study traces their history — from drama, the oldest of the arts on campus, to dance, the newest — as they slowly and painfully gained a foothold in American higher education. It also provides new information on the current state of the arts obtained from a survey of 17 institutions of widely varying size, control, and aspirations.

We would agree with Morrison that the arts are of crucial importance to society. For, as he says, "anyone involved or concerned with the development of our society today is simply not prepared to make informed choices and interpretations about cultural growth, decadent or healthy, if he is illiterate in the arts." Apparently many faculty and students agree with this judgment, for Morrison found in the institutions he surveyed a generally hospitable attitude among faculty toward the arts, and he predicts that class enrollments in the arts in the coming years "should go up at an above-normal rate of growth."

Much remains to be done, however, if the arts are to take their rightful place in American academic life. To this end, the author offers useful suggestions for consideration by American colleges and universities, including a commission for reordering the teaching of the arts, renewed community involvement, creation of "research and development" centers in the arts on the campuses, and a concerted effort to obtain support and funding at this institutional and national levels.

The author of this study has been a participant in the arts for over 35 years. His experienced and clear insights constitute a welcome contribution to our understanding of a subject seldom given the prominence it is due in deliberations about American higher education.

Clark Kerr

Chairman
The Carnegie Commission
on Higher Education

March 1973

Preface

When the Law of Parsimony is applied, an investigator is obliged to start with all the known truth and information available and then, by applying Occam's Razor, reveal the essentials in a practical investigation and determine the simplest explanation that accounts for all the facts. Since extensive information concerning the arts in colleges and universities does not yet exist, it is not possible now to provide this kind of full-fledged, lean explanation. Accordingly, this document represents a frankly personal, though judicious, probe into the growth of the arts on campus by a participant in that growth. Some hard evidence is available about the arts in higher education in the form of fallout from other studies, such as those on museums, on degrees earned, and on freshman norms. And some serious studies on "the arts" per se are beginning to appear. But no comprehensive study of the arts in academe has been done which would make possible debates such as those medicine has experienced on the training of "assistant physicians." If this present probe leads to such comprehensive studies of the arts in higher education, it will have served its major purpose.

The study begins with an essay on "The Case for the Arts in Higher Education," which explores the rationale for the arts in the curriculum.[1] Then, to set the stage for current developments, we provide historical brushups in the various arts—theater, dance, film, creative or poetic writing, music, visual arts, and architecture —as well as some comments on art museums, fine arts centers, and

---

[1] Concern here is directed to the question of *why* the arts should be an integral part of higher education, but not to the question of *how* or to the question of quality, *How well?*. Another report to the Commission (*Curriculum and Context: Essays on College Education,* edited by Carl Kaysen, to be published by McGraw-Hill Book Company in 1973) with a chapter on the arts by James Ackerman, will address itself, at least in part, to these questions.

"the concert series." We turn our attention next to national statistical surveys, some portions of which pertain to the arts. We then suggest the current status of the arts in profiles of 17 institutions of varying natures which have reported information on the arts on their campuses. Those familiar with higher education and the arts could probably suggest a half-dozen or so institutions for each of these 17 which would provide equally interesting and revealing conditions, but restrictions of time and expense limit this number. Those presented here, then, may be considered representative, not definitive, of the field; they were selected with a kind of knowledgeable arbitrariness. The following institutions were chosen:

Antioch College, Washington-Baltimore campus

Bennington College

Carnegie-Mellon University

Dartmouth College

Duke University

Earlham College

Fisk University

Harvard University

Indiana University

Jackson State College

New York University

Pasadena City College

Pennsylvania State University

University of California at Los Angeles

University of California at Santa Cruz

University of Georgia

University of New Mexico

We then discuss some of the issues arising from the responses made by these colleges and universities in comments on students, the resistance to and support for the rise of the arts in academe, and the rate of change in this rise. We close this probe of the rise of the arts in higher education today with a statement of possible future directions and recommendations.

Focus is on primal institutions in higher education rather than the complete postsecondary field. Thus, conservatories and strictly professional and commercial institutions are not represented. No study of the arts would be complete without the inclusion, for example, of Juilliard, the School of the Chicago Art Institute, and private studios in all the arts—including cosmetology—but that is beyond the purview of this investigation.

$\mathcal{A}$cknowledgments

What would one do without his colleagues? The many who contributed to this study were indispensable indeed. The primitive nature of information on the arts as well as the lack of an accepted taxonomy and suitable records put a premium on the understanding and cooperation of those answering my onerous questionnaire, and their help, as well as that of their institutions, is acknowledged with deep thanks. And those individuals interviewed were gracious in providing freely of their time and thoughtful responses. Among those who read and critiqued the manuscript, special appreciation is due Bernard Dukore, Michael Miller, Darragh Park, and Allen Sapp.

Joseph Anderson, Dorothy Madden, Norman Rice, and Frank Stillings were prompt and helpful in providing their unpublished manuscripts on film, dance, visual arts, and music, respectively.

The work of the U.S. Office of Education's National Center for Educational Statistics, the American Council on Education, and Noah Meltz of the University of Toronto is gratefully acknowledged. The International Council of Fine Arts Deans kindly permitted me to use data from the "in-house survey" I did for them in 1971.

Margaret Mahoney, James Ackerman, and Verne Stadtman expressed early interest in this project, and Clark Kerr's interest in the rise of the arts on the American campus and his specific thoughts on what would be useful to the Carnegie Commission on Higher Education were encouraging and vital in the formation of my approach to this probe into the nature of the arts in higher education.

Though not directly involved in the shaping of this report, but rather in the shaping of my thinking about a university and the arts in a university, three psychologists—Neal Miller, John Dollard, and Frank Barron—and three colleagues in the theater—the late

Kenneth Macgowan, Richard Schechner, and Marc Estrin—have been extremely influential. Their influence, arising out of informal dialogue through the last 35 years, has been challenging, stimulating, and supportive in diverse and subtle ways. I acknowledge them here to recognize my debt to the many, many students, colleagues, and professional artists and artisans who have developed the insights and judgments that are reflected throughout this report.

The support of my colleague, Kathryn Bloom, director of the Arts in Education Program of The JDR 3rd Fund, and through her interest, the support of the good offices of the Fund, were constant and indispensable.

The editorial assistance of Elaine Moss was a pleasure, as well as expert, and I owe much to her insight as well as her remarkable industry. And the secretarial attention of my personal secretary, Karen Schlitzer, to the project from the beginning was a contribution of great measure.

*The Rise of
the Arts on
the American Campus*

1. The Case for the Arts in Higher Education

The rise of the arts on the American campus is the result of a long and constant, if not consistent, battle of the natural inclination of human beings to sing, play, draw, paint, sculpt, write, and dance against the forces of puritanism, the work ethic, and the narrow scholasticism of the colonies and later of the United States. This battle still goes on.

On the campus, however, the tide of battle has turned for the arts and is unlikely to recede. My view is that the arts exist everywhere in nature if man is present, and that it was and is simply a matter of time for the arts, as one of the vital aspects of human endeavor, to become an integral part of higher education in balance with the sciences and technology, the social sciences, and the humanities. But since the arts are not dependent on higher education, the vital questions are these: Will higher education and the arts coexist vulgarly or beautifully—meaningfully or superficially? Will the arts be at the center of the university or on the periphery? In either case, what will be the effects on our society?

At the time the *Report of the Committee on the Visual Arts at Harvard University* (Harvard University, 1956) came out, I thought the case for the arts in higher education had been made once and for all by a working paper, "The Artist in the University," published as part of that report. This paper presented with strength and persuasion the position that "just as the scientist has found his place within the university, just as his laboratory has become academically respectable, so the artist and the studio, given time and opportunity, should find their places" (p. 48). This report, coupled with Susanne Langer's work and her particular observation that the discursive symbol does not encompass the full range of human expression, gave for me the intellectual rationale for the arts in the curriculum. More recently, and in addition to the above, psycholo

1

gists have clearly indicated that a fully functioning human being does not mature without the afferent as well as the cognitive, the emotional as well as the intellectual modes of learning.[1] Scientists like Glenn Seaborg (1968, pp. 28–46) have taken strong public positions in recent years for strengthening the arts "because of the complex needs of our creative and intellectual life." The preeminence of the arts in society may best be explained by this eloquent statement by Susanne Langer (1958, p. 1):

Every culture develops some kind of art as surely as it develops language. Some primitive cultures have no real mythology or religion, but all have some art, dance, song, design (sometimes only on tools or on the human body). Dance, above all, seems to be the oldest elaborated art.

The ancient ubiquitous character of art contrasts sharply with the prevalent idea that art is a luxury product of civilization, a cultural frill, a piece of social veneer.

It fits better with the conviction held by most artists, that art is the epitome of human life, the truest record of insight and feeling, and that the strongest military or economic society without art is poor in comparison with the savage painters, dancers, or idol-carvers. Wherever a society has really achieved culture (in the ethnological sense, not the popular sense of "social form") it has begotten art, not late in its career, but at the very inception of it.

Art is, indeed, the spearhead of human development, social and individual. The vulgarization of art is the surest symptom of ethnic decline. The growth of a new art or even a great and radically new style always bespeaks a young and vigorous mind, whether collective or single.

James Perkins (1965, pp. 671–678), in his inaugural address as president of Cornell University at Lincoln Center in 1965 entitled "The University and the Arts," said, however, that "the production of art and the performance of artistic work is *not* a fully accepted part of liberal education." History, yes—creation, no. Perkins' concern for effective ways of bringing the working artist onto the campus caused him to say, "Artists beware; but university prepare" (p. 678). This caveat applies to much of academe today, even where some of the arts exist in some strength. Where colleges and schools of the arts have been thoroughly established over a period

---

[1] Within the last two years, three universities have joined the University of Illinois in offering an undergraduate major in aesthetic education. They are Pennsylvania State University, the University of California at Santa Cruz, and the University of Massachusetts at Amherst.

of years,[2] at institutions like the University of Utah, Ohio University, and Syracuse University, they are an integral part of the university and suffer budget cuts and bonuses in concert with the rest of the academic areas, on the basis of merit and supply and demand. But generally, the state Perkins describes is still predominant.

The current thrust of students into the arts, however, is reordering curricular matters, course offerings, personnel changes, and budget support whether the time appears right or not. At one fairly young Eastern university, a department offering radio, TV, and film grew from no majors to 140 majors in two semesters. In fact, the "numbers game" that is on the side of the arts at the present time is a dangerous though welcome ally. With a burgeoning number of students and class enrollments to support the arts, there is less need for sound educational principles and more opportunity for empire building. Fortunately, many leaders are wise enough to use this development carefully in the interest of sound growth and quality work.

In Lima, Peru, in February of 1964, an extraordinarily illuminating colloquy developed in a symposium on "The Arts and the University" involving leaders of North and South American universities.[3] In a discussion between Clark Kerr, then president of the University of California, and the late physicist, J. Robert Oppenheimer, Kerr observed that creative talent is equally distributed in time and space and that, accordingly, the opportunity for that talent to take root and flower is offered or denied by the environment — in this case, the university environment. Franklin Murphy, then chancellor at the University of California at Los Angeles, responded with a statement that Oppenheimer and all accepted. After reviewing the difficulties and successes medicine, engineering, and architecture had experienced in making their ways into the university and the obstacles facing the arts in pursuing the same path, Murphy said, "I see in the precedents and in university history no reason why, if the will is there, the fine arts cannot be brought in as full and re-

[2] There are now 126 members of the International Council of Fine Arts Deans. To be a member of the council, an administrative officer must head a unit which includes two or more of the arts. All but a half dozen report that their function is understood by the university, that their work is appreciated in its own terms, and that their support is strong and fairly distributed.

[3] The symposium was called by the Council on Higher Education in the American Republics (1964).

spectable parts of the expanding, changing American university" (Council on Higher Education in the American Republics, 1964, p. 41). W. McNeil Lowry of the Ford Foundation followed by saying, "I think the university may finally become the patron of three-quarters of all that goes on in the arts in the United States" (p. 43).

At this writing, even with marked success in bringing the arts into many universities, some of the thinking and feeling of university faculties today does not reflect the spirit of that dialog in Lima. Some faculties have yet to see that universities hold the power to nurture and release all that talent which is equally distributed in time and space. A very real challenge exists for higher education — in coordination with all parts of the education chain from nursery school on (Bloom, 1971) — to provide the climate and opportunity for the artist to work and to develop, as it has done so successfully for the scientist, the engineer, and the physician and surgeon. Moreover, the student confrontations of the sixties and the current "cultural revolution," which is reordering the values of our society with emphasis on the "quality of life," have speeded up the demand for effective programs of the arts on campus. This condition, coupled with decreasing support for higher education, has created an arena in which the arts are presently determining the effectiveness and virility with which they will, or will not, take their place in academe. Conflict with the outworn, so-called traditional, views of the university and the constraints of "status quo" or austerity budgets are likely to leave neither middle ground nor time to turn around. Those institutions which have not made up their minds whether to encompass the arts fully or not are faced with the responsibility of making a statement which will reveal their values and their position in the current cultural revolution. There is even greater pressure on faculties and their leadership in the arts to change their respectable academic departments in a comfortable setting to active, restless, and productive forces on campus and off during this decade.

The problems are great. Some of them have been named by Margaret Mahoney.[4]

---

[4] These problems are stated in her chapter, "Overview of the Present," in *The Arts on Campus: The Necessity for Change,* edited by Margaret Mahoney (1970, pp. 22–25).

1   . . . The absolute separation of the arts, with very little evidence of inter-departmental cooperation or recognition of common interests.

2   . . . Little recognition that new ways may have to be found to reach large numbers of students, and that student differences, not only in aptitude but degree of interest, are relevant in planning an arts curriculum.

3   . . . The lack of relationship or coordination between the regular curriculum and the extra-curricular.

4   . . . The lack of correlation between curriculum planning and physical design of facilities for the arts.

5   . . . The failure to acknowledge that what goes on in elementary and secondary education is relevant to college teaching. The fault goes deeper because of the failure of colleges to take any responsibility, and thus any real interest in what the schools do and do not offer.

James Perkins (1965, p. 677) gives the following explanation of why the decision has not been made to bring the arts into the university as a fully professional discipline:

It has not been made because the scholar and artist still understand each other imperfectly. It has not been made because we have not really faced up to the costs of the special facilities that will be required. It has not been made because the universities have not yet seen the nature of the organizational arrangements that will be required. Or when they have seen them, they have not been bold enough to propose them and urge their adoption.

But the reordering of values in current thought meets us even in our daily newspapers (Lewis, 1972, op-ed page).

Like John Stuart Mill, those of this mind [those who recognize ecological necessity and take a more hopeful view of life] will think that a stable state is not only necessary but desirable—a society in which the mind and the arts would matter more than owning goods

If further argument is needed to bring all the arts full force into the mainstream of higher education, Daniel Bell (1970) has provided the rationale from the point of view of a sociologist. He has currently constructed an extremely interesting and provocative idea (p. 44).

American capitalism . . . has lost its traditional legitimacy which was based on a moral system of reward, rooted in a Protestant sanctification of work. It has substituted in its place a hedonism which promises a material ease and luxury, yet shies away from all the historic implications which a "voluptuary system"—and all its permissiveness and libertinism—implies.

. . . The characteristic style of an industrial society is based on the principles of economics and economizing. . . . Yet it is at this point that it comes into sharpest conflict with the cultural trends of the day, for the culture emphasizes anticognitive and anti-intellectual currents which are rooted in a return to instinctual modes.

In another context in the same article, he says, "Today culture has clearly become supreme; what is played out in the imagination of the artist foreshadows, however dimly, the social reality of tomorrow.[5]

This disjunction of society, according to Bell, has put the artist in a position to determine the nature of our culture, and he has done just that. What is important to the arts in higher education and in all education is not whether Bell is "right" or "wrong" about what the arts foreshadow, but his emphasis that the arts are vital, a sine qua non in the interpretation of our lives now and in future. Anyone involved in or concerned with the development of our society today is simply not prepared to make informed choices and interpretations about cultural growth, decadent or healthy, if he is illiterate in the arts. In his article, Bell mentions Joyce, Picasso, Braque, Schönberg, Ionesco, Beckett, Allen Ginzberg, and Woodstock. Who can enter this dialog without being able to "read" the nondiscursive symbols involved in the arts they represent?[6]

It is curious that the arts in American higher education, after some 300 years of waiting in the wings to get into the act—caroling outside the president's house waiting to be invited in for punch and cookies—are only now seriously recognized as a key, as a prime mover, in education and society.

[5] In November 1971, a paper by the author entitled "The Arts as Early Warning Signals" appeared in *Arts in Society* (Morrison, 1971, pp. 469–477). This paper presented the view that "there is now a growing awareness of the non-cognitive, the non-discursive symbol, the feelings, what the Latin Americans call the spirit" (ibid., p. 469) and that society is turning to the artist for leadership in this encounter.

[6] Maybe we need a lexicon for nondiscursive symbols!

2. Historical Sketches

If we look back into history we can see the arts—in different places and in different ways—moving from the periphery to the heart of the campus and infiltrating the curriculum. A separate look at each of the arts during the course of their infiltration gives a sense of how this developed, documents the growth, and provides a historical base for the current scene and some appreciation of the rate of change. Because theater and dance drew somewhat more attention and certainly more invective than art and music, sketches of their development are given first. Note in the rise of all the arts an increasing involvement on the campus at the turn of the century, a noticeable acceleration between the two world wars, and a strong upsurge after World War II, particularly around 1960. At this writing, the crest of this growth in the arts may not yet have been reached, which makes for speculation and a need for better forecasting.

THEATER Some interest in the drama was present at Harvard at the end of the seventeenth century, as President Increase Mather made a note in his diary on October 10, 1698, that he had "examined the Scholars about the comedy, etc." A "pastoral colloquy" in 1702 at William and Mary and a performance in 1736 by "the young gentlemen of the Colledge" of "the tragedy of Cato" are generally considered to be the first dramatic performances by American college students. But criticism of plays was also present in this period. Writing to the Overseers of Harvard College in 1723, Cotton Mather expressed an attitude which was to be held by many in the next 250 years:

NOTE: In this section on theater I relied heavily on Wallace (1954); particularly John L. Clark's chapter, "Educational Dramatics in Nineteenth Century Colleges" (pp. 521–551); and Clifford Eugene Hamar's chapter, "College and University Theatre Instruction in the Early Twentieth Century" (pp. 572–594).

"Whether the scholars have not their studies filled with books which may truly be called *Satan's Library.* Whether the books mostly read among them are not plays, novels, empty and vicious pieces of poetry" (Quincy, 1860, vol. I, p. 559). State and church would repeatedly band together to keep these satanic forces in check.

To be sure, a case had been made for the theater in England by William Gager, the Christ College dramatist who answered an attack by Dr. John Rainolds of Owen College in 1592. Gager (Boas, 1914, pp. 235–36, 241) responded with a rationale that braved the Atlantic crossing and is still used today.

We contrarwise doe it [produce plays] to recreate owre selves, owre House, and the better part of the Vniversitye, with some learned Poem or other; to practyse owre owne style eyther in prose or verse; to be well acquantyed with *Seneca* or *Plautus. . . .* your goodwill I doe and ever will most gladly embrace, and your judgment toe, in this cause so farr, as you wryte in the generall agaynst Histriones.

Gager's argument for theater on the educational grounds that it fosters the development of individual talent and imparts knowledge of the great works of the past continues to be the basic rationale for all the arts on the campus today.

The diary kept by Nathaniel Ames of Harvard in 1761 indicates increased interest in plays. He notes seeing *Cato* performed twice in July of 1758, seeing *The Orphan* the following year, and playing in *The Recruiting Officer* himself that year. In 1765, however, Ames enters this note: "Scholars punished at College for acting over the great and last day in a very shocking manner, personating the Jude eterat Devil, etc." (Matthews, 1914, p. 295).

The drama appeared in the forms of "academical exercises," extracurricular endeavor, and playwriting by faculty and students for commencements and "dialogues." Apparently there was some lessening of interest in the early part of the nineteenth century, or perhaps drama was attracting less attention, but activities in theater continued. By 1844 the Hasty Pudding Club at Harvard had emerged. It was described as "a rather jolly amalgam of literary, convivial, and patriotic elements" and "theatrical representations," and it served as a prototype for the development of extracurricular dramatics in other colleges and universities.

Harvard's historian, Samuel Eliot Morison, observed that "from the Civil War to the World War, Harvard undergraduates had an insatiable thirst for theatricals." This enthusiasm, moreover, was not restricted to the Harvard campus, but developed in extracurricular productions all over the country. The expansion of the railroad brought professional companies to campuses and communities in all quarters of the country. The "musical burlesque," written and staged by clubs, gave a currency to a kind of populist theater. Language faculties began to sponsor foreign language classics. This was the period when "the Greek play" became an annual, carefully prepared event on many campuses.

Soon the theater was respectable enough for universities to invite professionals for lectures. Steele MacKaye appeared at Princeton in the 1870s, lecturing on "The Mystery of Emotion and its Expression in Art." Henry Irving was at Harvard in 1884–85 and Joseph Jefferson was at the University of Michigan in 1897. By the turn of the century, or about 200 years after plays were considered at Harvard as part of "Satan's Library," hostility to theater had been allayed, and acted drama was eyeing a place in the sanctity of the curriculum.

Thomas Dickinson gave a short-lived course on the "staging of plays" at Baylor in 1901–02, but George Pierce Baker is generally credited as the first American professor to be concerned with "living theater." In a personal note to the author, Kenneth Macgowan wrote:

Baker gave his playwriting course, first at Radcliffe, in the spring of 1904. He did not give it at Harvard until the spring of 1906.

The 47 Workshop also began at Radcliffe. The first performance, directed by Sam Hume, while Baker was in Europe, was in January, 1913. It was made possible by the Radcliffe 47 Club, which raised $500. English 47 did not teach anything about the physical production of plays, though Baker may have mentioned the differences between the playhouses and methods of various periods.

In 1925 when Baker left the Harvard 47 Workshop to set up a new department of drama at Yale, New York columnist Heywood Broun wrote:

YALE   47

HARVARD   0

"Bootlegging" of theater into the curriculum characterized most of the growth of theater in higher education through World

War II. Public Speaking 2 a-b, for example, was often a euphemism for "acting." The next step was an omnibus "play production" course deemed necessary for theater training. Exceptions to this included the drama department at Carnegie Institute of Technology (began in 1914), Alexander Drummond's work at Cornell, the theater concentration in speech at Northwestern, and E. C. Mabie's program at Iowa University.

In 1936 in St. Louis, Mabie organized the American Educational Theatre Association (AETA—now the American Theatre Association) as a separate section of the National Association of Teachers of Speech. Mabie had also been a key figure in the development of the National Theatre Conference (founded in 1931, reorganized with membership limited in 1936), which encouraged foundation support for college and community theaters. By 1949, AETA had developed the talent, experience, and funds to launch its own major publication, the *Educational Theatre Journal.* Thus, at the midpoint of the twentieth century, the theater in colleges and universities may be said to have established itself on its own terms. Diversity and functionalism still existed, but the theater had brought itself into academe in the short 250 years since President Mather's diary entry of 1698.

In 1960 AETA published for the first time the *Directory of American College Theatre,* edited by Burnet Hobgood. In 1967 Richard Ayers brought out a second edition, which is the most recent overview of the field. He reports that of 1,581 regionally accredited United States colleges and universities, 30 percent (574) offer degrees in theater as a field of study. Although the data are only partially complete, an annual audience of approximately 5 million witnesses to 10,000 reported productions is indicated. There were 116,000 enrolled students in formal classrooms and another 100,000 students involved in putting on plays. Of the schools offering these programs 43 percent describe themselves as providing a liberal arts education and 10.5 percent attest to liberal arts training with a vocational bent. Another 43 percent describe their motives as recreational and avocational and 3.5 percent classify them as professional-commercial.

In the seven years between the first and second editions of the *Directory* (from 1960 to 1967), the number of undergraduate majors tripled from about 5,500 to 18,000 and the number of courses offered for credit increased from 7,000 to 12,000. In 1967 there were 168 institutions offering the master's degree and 38 offering the doctorate. Since 1960 twenty more programs at the graduate level have been added. About 3,000 graduate degrees were awarded each year between 1960 and 1967.

At present many efforts are underway to raise the standards of work in the field and to "professionalize" certain programs. A division of the American Theatre Association, the University Repertory Theatre Association, has sprung up to develop graduate theater companies and to professionalize them at the grass roots level. The League for Professional Theatre Training, composed of 11 institutions, is more selective and emphasizes high-quality work. These are manifestations of deep concern that college theater should have a closer liaison with the professional theater, a view strongly stated by both professionals and academic theater men in a special 1966 issue of the *Educational Theatre Journal,* "The Relationship Between Educational Theatre and Professional Theatre."

Another development is the emergence of a small, but forceful group of younger faculty who are concerned with a wider use of theater at all levels of education. Plays, traveling troupes, curricular materials, and teacher training for grades kindergarten through 12 are being developed for the classroom teacher and the orchard-run of children, as well as for the talented and motivated student.

From its center—the liberal arts, avocational base of most offerings in higher education—the field, then, is moving in two directions: (1) toward the professionalizing of work at the highest levels of artistry in both established and experimental areas and (2) toward the professionalizing of theater education for the schools, kindergarten through twelfth grade (Graham, 1966).

A development in the experimental area which appears likely to influence the field is that which is sometimes called "anthropological theater," a mode which is closer to dance. It is based on an approach to theater in its fundamental, ritualistic relationships to man's daily life and expressive behavior. "Political theater" and "street theater" are current manifestations. Some young practitioners of the art are currently of the view that they will never return to the formal or traditional theater. Whatever the outcome, groups such as the Bread and Puppet Theater based at Goddard College are the antithesis of "elitist theater" as seen in conventional buildings of the establishment on the campus. These groups are likely to bring the theater closer to the more intimate, humanized experience which the "primitive ring" used to provide for tribal events. At the same time, an effort to create a similar, personalized encounter with theater by means of technology and multimedia is also at work. Hopefully, the campus will provide a receptive, useful laboratory not only for experiment in form and technique, but also for free play of expressive behavior in the theater which reflects the hopes, passions, and problems of our society.

DANCE   Dance, it turns out, was not thought to be all bad by the founders of New England. In 1625, before coming to Massachusetts from England, the Reverend John Cotton wrote:

> Dancing (yea though mixt) I would not simply condemn. For I see two sorts of mixt dancings in use with God's people in the Old Testament, the one religious, Exod. XV, 20, 21; the other civil, tending to the praise of conquerors, as the former of God, I. Sam. XVII, 6, 7. Only lascivious dancing to wanton ditties, and amorous gestures and wanton dalliances, especially after feasts, I would bear witness against, as a great *flabella libidinis* (in Marks, 1957, p. 15).

In 1628 William Bradford attacked the Maypole, calling it a "stynching idol" around which heathens worshipped. But early theorists of education in England such as Sir Thomas Elyot in 1531, John Milton in *Tractate on Education* in 1644, and John Locke in *Some Thoughts Concerning Education* in 1690, saw dance as part of education. Locke wrote:

> Dancing, being that which gives *graceful Motions* all the Life, and above all things Manliness, and a becoming Confidence to Young Children, I think cannot be learned too early. . . . it gives Children manly Thought and Carriage, more than any thing (ibid., p. 17).

In 1687 an instructor at Harvard wrote in *Compendium Physicae* that, despite abuse by man's corruption, the gymnastic arts, which include dancing, were invented and taught for the regulating of poise.

In Virginia, dancing was prohibited on the Sabbath, but proponents of aristocratic education expected a gentleman to dance well. In Philadelphia in 1706, the Society of Friends agreed that "Friends are generally grieved that a dancing and fencing school are tolerated in this place." The Shakers, however, who arrived

NOTE: This section on dance is based on an unpublished manuscript by Dorothy Madden (1972), chairman of the department of dance at the University of Maryland, and *America Learns to Dance,* by Joseph E. Marks, III (1957).

in this country near the beginning of the Revolutionary War, had definite dance patterns as part of their worship. Others considered dance to be part of their children's education. The Kent County School in Chestertown, Maryland, advertised in 1745 that "young gentlemen may be instructed in fencing and dancing by very good masters" as well as being taught Greek, Latin, writing, and arithmetic. Thomas Jefferson scheduled dancing for his daughter from ten o'clock to one o'clock every day, and President Edward Holyoke of Harvard College noted in his diary that he had paid a Mr. Turner for dancing lessons for his daughter Peggy. Plain people and blacks danced for the fun of it at bees and frolics.

Despite this evident interest in dancing in the eighteenth century, however, there was a movement toward the end of that century and into the nineteenth by leaders in higher education and the church to keep dancing off the campus, as well as out of commencement and other college exercises. This effort was sustained by such forces as the Great Revival of 1858, during which tracts appeared under such titles as "The Social Evils of Dancing, Card Playing, and Theatre-Going." In general, this spirit kept dance out of colleges and universities throughout the nineteenth century, but it was always a seesaw battle and, in some places, dance was encouraged and developed. Harvard had licensed a dancing school in 1815, and Jefferson had suggested that dance be included in the curriculum at the University of Virginia because it was one of the arts that "embellished life." The University of North Carolina banned any dancing. William and Mary followed the more liberal views of English colleges and maintained that the college had to offer dance if it were to compete with English schools for the education of aristocratic gentlemen. President Moses Wadell of the University of Georgia banished dance, but it quickly returned on his retirement.

Dance began to appear as a form of exercise in private schools. Emma Willard brought dance into Middlebury College and later into her Troy Female Seminary. Catherine Beecher introduced it at the Hartford Female Seminary, as did Mary Lyon at Mount Holyoke Seminary. In each case, dance was part of an exercise program. The nose of the camel under the tent of respectability was the act of providing music for "light calisthenics." In 1869 Matthew Vassar told his board of trustees at Vassar College, "I heartily approve of [dancing]." The period after the Civil War saw further incorporation of dance into schools and colleges as part of physical education.

The do-si-do between dance and American higher education continued until 1917, when Margaret D'Houbler drove a salient into the fields of academe with an educational concept of dance as art, no longer limited to recreational and "genteel" social exercises. After studying with professionals in New York, Miss D'Houbler returned to the University of Wisconsin in 1917 with the idea of teaching a truly educational dance form and offered the first program in dance as an art experience. By 1926 the university had approved the first major dance curriculum, and dance had caught on in academe. By 1948 Walter Terry reported that at least 105 colleges and universities offered dance and that 92 gave academic credit for it. In 1969 the National Dance Division of the American Association of Health, Physical Education, and Recreation reported that 110 institutions gave a major or concentration in dance. Of these, 22 were in separate departments, 6 in theatre, 5 in fine arts, and 77 in physical education—the trend being away from physical education toward identification of dance as such. Forty-two institutions offered the master's degree and six the doctorate. In 1962 New York University awarded the first Ph.D. for choreography as a performing art. The "dissertation" was presented in concert form.

An important aspect of this growth was the close relationship that grew up in the 1930s between higher education and New York professionals, particularly Hanya Holm, Charles Weidman, Doris Humphrey, Martha Graham, and Louis Horst. Bennington College, with Martha Hill at the helm, gave direction to efforts to use the talents of mature artists throughout the country, and the world of education today continues to be injected with the drive of the professional world. This healthy relationship was emphasized and encouraged by a Developmental Conference on the Dance sponsored by the Arts and Humanities Program of the U.S. Office of Education in 1968 (Dance . . . , 1968). The result of combined professional and academic effort is that offerings in the schools now include techniques (various modern styles, ballet, and jazz) at all levels, extensive courses in choreography, repertory, rhythmic training, music for dance, music ethnic forms, notation, aesthetics, theory and philosophy, history, theater, dance therapy, methods teaching, and dance for children. Twelve states now recognize a special teaching certificate for dance in their public schools.

Research in dance has been supported by private and federal grants, and the Committee on Research on Dance (CORD) has held five conferences. The Dance Collection of the New York Public

Library in Lincoln Center has become the most significant repository for dance in the world. One result of the concern for and study of what some people call the oldest art form is that folk dancing, taught by rote as "exercises" in the twenties, is now taught as dance in terms of folk art and ethnic art, as expressive of cultures. Indeed, Alan Lomax's current worldwide research in "choreometrics" finds that cultures may be identified by their dance forms.

As the newest of the arts to be included in higher education, dance has been less concerned than the others with academic partitioning and territorial prerogatives and is developing its genuine concerns with society as well as developing itself as a rigorous art form. Since 1959, in the company of the other arts as a constituent member of the National Council of the Arts in Education (now the American Council for the Arts in Education), dance has championed the right of each human being to experience art in some form compatible with his interests and abilities. In fact, many consider dance and film not only as forms which are in current vogue, but also as forms which are strongly contributing to the revitalization of the arts on campus today.

FILM Film began to appear in university courses during the 1920s. Several schools take credit for offering the "first" course. Most of these courses were of the "Introduction to Motion Pictures" type, organized along the broadest lines of art appreciation with some history and some discussion of nontechnical techniques. After 50 years, the general introductory course remains today the most widespread of film courses in the United States, with approximately 800 such courses offered in almost as many colleges.

The first major in film was offered in 1932 by the University of Southern California, which began a master's program in cinema in 1935 and established one of the first Ph.D. programs in film-related work. These USC offerings, like many today, are in a communications framework. The first full-fledged scholarly film program with a Ph.D. was established by New York University in 1970.

Expansion of film studies did not begin until the postwar years. The following institutions pioneered the various contexts in which major programs in film were to be offered:

NOTE· This section on film is based on a unpublished manuscript by Joseph Anderson (1972), director of the film program at Ohio University.

University	Year film program established	Area
Indiana University	1944	Audio-visual/Instructional materials
New York University	1946	Broadcast/Radio-TV
University of California at Los Angeles	1947	Theater
Boston University	1947	Communications

The following figures indicate the growth of the total number of film courses (including all courses strongly concerned with film in any academic context) in the United States from 1946 to 1959:

Year	Number of courses
1946	86
1949	113
1953	161
1957	275
1959	305

The major growth in film, however, occurred in the sixties; film in the university is basically a product of this decade. In 1959 only 10 programs around the country offered undergraduate majors in film. In 1971, 47 offered degrees in film, ranging from the A.A. to the Ph.D., with approximately 4,600 undergraduate majors and 1,500 graduate majors in M.A., M.S., M.F.A., and Ph.D. programs. Degrees in cinema, motion pictures, film, and radio-TV-film are now definitely "in." Ninety-six universities without formal film programs in 1971 had students majoring in film, though actually taking their degrees in other subjects. Four hundred and twenty-seven colleges and universities offered more than one course in film. A total of 2,400 courses in film in 1971 compares with 850 courses in 1964.

Between 1916 and 1969, 493 theses and dissertations were presented whose prime subject was film. Of this number, 104 were Ph.D. dissertations, a very large majority of which (at least 70 percent in recent years and 95 percent a decade or more ago) were on the various pedagogic uses of film and often involved statistical research on the effectiveness of instructional films. The first thesis — presented at the University of Iowa in 1916 — was on teaching with movies.

Most film programs, even large ones, do not exist as separate administrative entities, but are usually under the jurisdiction of a "large" discipline. If the film curriculum is large, it is usually an area in broadcasting/communications or theater/drama. Over 40 percent of all film curricula in the country are in one or the other of these two administrative units. If a film program is smaller, it may be located anywhere, but the tendency is to locate it in arts/fine arts departments. About 20 percent of all film programs are in this administrative unit. The next largest area of control is English, which contains about 10 percent of all programs. Independent film departments/schools account for only 5 percent of the national total of film curricula. In short, the "controlling context" for film is seldom film itself, but some other discipline.

A major characteristic of film curricula is that they tend to be developed in the widest variety of administrative/academic contexts. In addition to the large areas described above, major film programs are organized within the following disciplines: speech, journalism, instructional media, photography, design, theology/religion, and humanities. Important courses and some programs in film are also found in the areas of political science, foreign language, American studies, engineering, anthropology, social ecology, music, comparative literature, and architecture.

In the past three years there has been an apparent slowdown in the development of major programs in film. The primary trend during this period has been the appearance of film in the curricula of smaller colleges, particularly those with a "liberal" liberal arts context. Here, the tendency is to open a film course or two in the art department, where the teacher of the film course doubles in other media, primarily photography, mixed media, printmaking, painting, drawing, and design.

Film offerings can be classified into four major categories:

1   *Appreciation/history/general/introduction/film and . . . courses* This is historically the oldest category and is today, as it always has been, the most widespread. Most often the courses have unlimited enrollment and serve both as general education courses for all majors and as the beginning of the major sequence for film majors. It is almost always a service course and, as such, the "rent payer," because enrollments are large. The average enrollment in a course of this type (according to data from a survey that

includes the spectrum of courses from the largest universities to the smaller colleges) is 200 students. Enrollment in a *single* course of this kind is, in several instances, up to 500. This large enrollment indicates student interest and reflects the high costs of such a course, for which films must be rented. (Budgets for one course of this type range from $200 to $1,500.)

2   *Elementary production, usually with film as a studio art*   This is often the 8mm course. Emphasis is on personal exploration, on film as a means of personal expression. There is a wide range of course objectives, but all are nonprofessional. Only the most basic techniques are taught and only simple equipment is used. In a broadcasting/radio-TV context, this course would be in 16mm, with emphasis on news and simple "documentary" shooting. On a number of campuses, this kind of activity is available only on an extracurricular basis without credit, though some campuses offer it on both a curricular and noncurricular basis. In recent years, this kind of course has shown the most rapid expansion. Enrollment averages 35 but can go as high as 90.

3   *Professional production*   These courses are the core of most professional programs. They are very expensive to run because of equipment costs. In some courses, materials (raw stock, processing) are furnished to students at no extra cost to them. Some of these subsidies go as high as $500 in advanced courses. The recent tendency, which is spreading, however, is to cut back on subsidies by requiring students to pay for materials. The early practice of organizing the major curriculum in sharply defined, almost "trade" areas such as sound recording, editing, etc., is decreasing. Production courses are becoming broader based, with more emphasis on developing many skills simultaneously and approaching the ideal of the "total filmmaker." This is part of a shift in emphasis away from "job training" for industry and dramatic films and toward imagist, noncommercial films and films as documentary. The average production course has 30 students (graduate or undergraduate) though in a few places enrollments go up to 60 students.

4   *Scholarly courses*   These are advanced courses which deal with historical aspects of film, theory, and criticism. These courses, more than those of other categories, conform to the traditional structuring of college courses. The main emphasis is on criticism; the secondary concern is review of film theory. History is also widely reviewed, but there is little emphasis on researching and writing original history.

In addition to professional production, the teaching of films as an artistic medium, and/or the scholarly directions of film work in universities, a major development in the past two years has been the formation of courses (and full curricula) for preparing teachers of film for secondary schools. Over 100 colleges and universities offer courses especially designed for "film teachers." The number of such courses has doubled in the past three years.

In 1971 there were approximately 300 full-time and 333 part-time faculty members in departments offering a major in film. Altogether about 1,600 persons teach film in American universities and colleges, with a greater prevalence of part-time teachers than in many other academic areas. Over 50 percent of the people teaching film full time have no "film degree," but majored in some other subject. This is particularly true of people who have been teaching for the past 10 years, with the film degree holder almost nonexistent among senior faculty — as is typical of the early developmental stage of any emerging academic discipline. There is presently a heavily accelerated "Ph.D-ization" of film teaching. This move includes the production area, where there is an increasing number of teachers from academically oriented programs rather than from "studio" arts. Thus, a small segment of people who teach production never practiced, but only studied it.

The major professional organizations are (1) the University Film Association, founded in 1947, with approximately 350 members, over half of whom are not teaching but work in film production on the campus, making sponsored educational films; and (2) the Society for Cinema Studies, founded in 1959. This is the major scholarly society for film, with a membership of approximately 120. Membership is open by invitation only and candidacy is reviewed and voted on by members. The College Art Association, the American Theatre Association, and the Speech Association of America have component parts concerned with film or have at one time or another expressed interest in problems of film teaching.

Several resource organizations exist. The American Film Institute, founded in 1967, acts as a clearinghouse in certain film education activities, runs special shows in Washington, D.C., theaters, and is trying to work with film archives. It is active in cataloging and publishing basic reference works in film and also runs a "training and research center" on the West Coast for 40 young people with either film making or scholarly film interests. This program is roughly equal in standards to most of the major graduate film programs in American universities but is perhaps more closely tied with the Hollywood film industry. The American Federation of Film Societies has a membership of about 500, which is approximately one-eighth of the total number of film societies in the United States, most of which are college-related. These societies provide key showings of important films for their respective campuses. Almost every United States campus has one or more film series or society, and frequently these groups serve as beachheads for the formal introduction of film into the curriculum. The major film archives are at the Library of Congress in Washington, D.C., the Museum of Modern Art in New York City, and the George Eastman House in Rochester, New York. Their respective holdings are extensive, but even collectively neither their efforts nor their resources are equivalent to peer groups in other countries.

Resources and the costs thereof are a major problem in film. In scholarly areas, films themselves are the prime resource material. But prints are expensive, and no college library can acquire them the way they acquire books, not only because of the expense but also because of copyright problems and the unavailability of prints. More prints of more films for more showings over longer lending periods for vastly cheaper rates are greatly needed. Many schools with film programs do have extensive book collections. A "good" collection of books on film numbers about 1,000 volumes. Basic older works have been reprinted extensively.

Costs of equipment and materials for production courses are also high. The average cost of a film thesis for an M.F.A. is about $900.

The recent "leveling" in university income and enrollments could lead to some setbacks for film, which is still a somewhat suspect subject in many college curricula. Film is especially vulnerable because of (1) the high costs of its programs, (2) its recent establishment in most cases (universities may operate on a last-in, first-out basis), and (3) questions of academic tradition and justification.

As far as the discipline itself is concerned, there is a need for clarification of student interests and societal possibilities in the different areas within the subject and a need for a better understanding of what kind of balance between the following is possible and desirable:

1 *Film as part of general education* Here elementary experience in film making and moderate investigation of the academic aspects of film are provided in a context in which production courses are parallels of basic creative writing courses, even of basic "expression" courses such as English Composition. Emphasis is on communication, reaching out, expression, with film serving as an alternative or additional means to create, inform, show, and feel. There is also concern for "appreciation"—getting to know more about film.

2 *Film as yet another medium available to the studio artist* who senses the limitations of one medium breaking down and requires skills and experience in order to expand his total range of art tools. This trend involves film in all kinds of mixed media developments and events.

3 *Film as a major subject for professionally oriented students* Here there are points of tension between acquiring skills and training for existing job descriptions in the "industry" and acquiring skills needed for following a more personal vision. What kind of balance should there be between a background of skills and a body of personal work? Also, should the old nineteenth-century, but still overwhelming, idea of art as intimate, personal, internalized, individual creation be de-emphasized in favor of work that attempts more directly to reach out?

4 *Film as a subject of scholarly concern* Scholarly work is being done in film by students and established scholars, but is still uneven in both cases. Comparative studies, particularly those related to literary concerns, are dominant. Film historiography is very poor. There is yet no fully adequate general textbook of film history, and even specialized works on film history are weak. Structural analysis is rising as a critical method and seems promising.

Film cannot escape connections with other arts — and with other cultures. Some new definition of *medium* is needed, as film is often too sharply defined. Perhaps, as with other established media, film needs to be looked at not as a total profession, trade, subject, discipline, or medium — not as a thing complete in itself with its own rules — but rather as one of many possible means to work with moving pictures.

CREATIVE OR POETIC WRITING Writing has always been part of instruction in English, whether it meant teaching the skills of expository prose or encouraging students to express their own imaginings. Special classes gradually evolved in various schools in which the prime focus was on making works of art with words. Often these classes have been called *creative writing* courses, though perhaps this term does not adequately capture the distinctive spirit of the endeavor; when a biologist writes up the results of his research, for example, his writing may be new and creative. Perhaps "poetic writing" better expresses the artistic connotations involved in making something new with words alone, though in this case novels, short stories, and graffiti, as well as poetry, would be considered poetic. At any rate, there is a growing awareness on the campus that creative writing is as much an art as sculpture or dance.

Only recently has there been a movement to identify university writing programs with the other arts.[1] In 1967 Charles D. Wright of the University of North Carolina was the first *literary* artist ever invited to speak to a conference of the National Council of the Arts in Education. In addition, only recently have there been efforts to identify creative writing programs within the offerings of English departments and to form a national professional association of these programs. An organization called Associated Writing Programs was established in the last half of the sixties and now has between 50 and 60 affiliated member institutions. The following are the objectives of this association, as expressed by its founder, novelist R. V. Cassill of Brown University (cited in Wright, 1967, p. 38):

1 To set up a clearinghouse (or agency) to place writers more usefully and profitably in the mainstream of literary education. . . .

2 To build a new publishing and reading community within the academic community, among the academic multitudes. . . .

3 To support and define the M.F.A. as a terminal degree for those whose primary and long-term commitment to letters is a commitment to writing and its relevant disciplines.

Originally the association affiliated only institutions with some type of graduate program in creative writing, but in 1971 it began to accept members with only undergraduate work, including community colleges.

In 1968 the College English Association, with the cooperation of the Book-of-the-Month Club, published for the first time a *Directory of Creative Writing Programs in the United States and Canada.* This directory and the second edition, which was published in 1970, provide listings of creative writing programs that are within English departments in four-year institutions. (Expository and technical writing courses are excluded.) In 1968 there were 680 such programs with 491 full-time and 920 part-time faculty members. In 1970 there were 817 programs with 543 full-time and 1,245 part-time faculty members. In 1970, 27 institutions sponsored or hosted writers' conferences and summer workshops.

---

[1] When the Institute of American Indian Arts was created at Santa Fe, New Mexico, eight years ago, the Indian staff simply installed creative writing as one of the arts without much ado.

Thirty-seven institutions offered an undergraduate major or concentration in creative writing, fifty-eight offered graduate programs in creative writing or a creative M.A. thesis option, and four offered Ph.D. programs. Two hundred and forty-two schools had a writer-in-residence of some type. Well-established programs, to name only a few, exist at the University of Iowa, San Francisco State, Johns Hopkins, Indiana University, Boston University, the University of Oregon, and the University of North Carolina at Greensboro.

Needless to say, there are many additional creative writing courses in two-year colleges and also outside English departments. Sometimes, though rarely, writing is part of an interdisciplinary fine arts program. Sometimes it is an elective within a school of journalism. Sometimes it is in a department of radio, TV, and film or in a theater department. The dimensions of these offerings are as yet unknown.

This appearance of creative writing in a variety of areas points out, however, the obvious fact that writing is deeply related to many of the other arts. In his 1967 address to the Conference on the Arts in Education, Charles Wright (1967, p. 42) said, "I think a creative writing program is most likely to flourish when it is part of a large and varied involvement in the arts on a campus. . . . Though it is hard to measure, there is a kind of symbiosis by which creative writing thrives on a campus."

MUSIC Beginning in the Middle Ages, the stewardship, support, and thrust for the dissemination and influence of music gradually shifted from the church to the aristocracy. In the last century, the conservatory briefly but intensely took over these functions, and today they have been assumed, for the greater part, by the universities.

Music was, of course, one subject of the quadrivium, and by the end of the Middle Ages it had been assigned a singular place in the curricula of some Western universities. The Oxford statutes of 1431 give such an indication. Cambridge granted a bachelor of music degree as early as 1463, Oxford as early as 1499.

Limited evidence exists of music study in American institutions of education in the first 100 years of their existence. That music

NOTE: This section on music is based on an unpublished manuscript by Frank S. Stillings (1972), dean of the School of Fine and Applied Arts at Central Michigan University.

was a part of college study at Harvard is implied in a tract written by a graduate of 1698.

The musical societies, singing societies, and musical clubs of communal life migrated to the campuses during the latter part of the eighteenth century. By 1800 performing organizations were sufficiently numerous for one to conclude that they were a normal, expected part of college life. Records of significant university events, principally commencement programs, provide evidence of such groups at the University of Pennsylvania, Harvard, Yale, Dartmouth, et al. Enigmatically, music, which was firmly implanted at Oxford as a part of academe with a faculty of its own by the end of the Middle Ages, did not develop in the United States as an appropriate instructional subject in higher education until the latter part of the nineteenth century.

The earliest instruction in music at the normal school, college, and university in this country was in vocal music. This early training, which appeared first in normal schools, served the purpose of preparing students to teach music, but the emphasis was on music as a cultural study. From about 1835 to 1870, as music appeared at the collegiate level, efforts were consistently directed toward making music an integral part of the curriculum by convincing students and administrations of the instructional values of music.

In 1835, one year after vocal music was officially introduced into the Boston public schools, the normal school at Lexington, Massachusetts, provided opportunities for vocal music study. Within the next 10 years, offerings in music appeared at three other normal schools in the Northeast—at Westfield, Massachusetts; Bridgewater, Massachusetts; and Albany, New York. By 1835, Oberlin College had a professor of sacred music and 30 years later the conservatory was established. Harvard was offering lectures in music by 1862, but not until 1870 were courses offered on a regular basis (i.e., providing credit for degree programs). In that year, a course in the history of music and elective courses in harmony and counterpoint were available. Vassar College provided music courses as early as 1867, and by 1872 eight of its forty-two instructors were teaching music.

Concomitantly, conservatories developed rapidly and abundantly. The movement began with the establishment of a conservatory at East Greenwich, Rhode Island, in 1859 and one in Providence a little later. The Oberlin Conservatory, as mentioned, was founded in 1865. The New England Conservatory, organized in

1867, was incorporated in 1870. The year 1867 was a rich one for the development of musical culture in the United States. Founded in that year, along with the New England Conservatory, were the Boston Conservatory, the Chicago Musical College, and the Cincinnati Conservatory. Within the following 20 years, other outstanding conservatories were formed, including the Dana Musical Institute, the Detroit Conservatory, the College of Music of Cincinnati, the New York College of Music, the Cleveland Conservatory, and the American Conservatory of Chicago. Several of these schools still provide the musical world with some of its most respected professional musicians.

By 1915, music as an academic discipline had been accepted by colleges and universities across the United States. Departments, schools, and colleges of music had evolved into established units within private and public institutions of higher education. All state universities with any degree of sophistication had such units. Music as culture and method had blossomed lavishly on campuses; from extracurricular activities of vocal and instrumental performance music grew to full recognition at the collegiate level for the development of the performer, historian, and educator.

During the upsurge of collegiate departments of music and conservatories, many independent schools appeared under the title "conservatory." Some truly deserved the distinction of the title, but many were one-room, one-person entities totally unworthy of such distinction. The same conditions prevailed in varying degrees on campuses. Fortunately, the Depression of the thirties took a heavy toll among these conservatories of lesser standards. Unfortunately, the Depression led to the bankruptcy of some conservatories which were contributing significantly to musical culture. Depressed conditions, along with spiraling operational costs in the 1940s, closed virtually all remaining major conservatories except the most financially stalwart and those allied with institutions of higher education.

The disparate quality of music offerings and the disparate content of curricula in both conservatories and departments of music had led in 1927 to the formation of a national accrediting agency, the National Association of Schools of Music (NASM). As a result of the work of NASM, definable standards exist and, although curricula and degrees vary, a national norm has developed.

Accredited Institutions of Higher Education, 1971–72, published for the Federation of Regional Accrediting Commissions of Higher

Education by the American Council on Education, lists 1,999 accredited universities, colleges, and junior colleges. An estimated 1,500 have music in some form. NASM's *Music in Higher Education, 1970–71,* a summary of information from the annual reports of member institutions, indicates enrollments of 45,333 undergraduate music majors, 6,167 master's level students, and 1,724 doctoral candidates. The summary indicates that these data represent reports of 287 member institutions from a total of 385. During the same reporting period *Students Enrolled for Advanced Degrees,* issued by the Office of Education of the U.S. Department of Health, Education and Welfare, indicated that 8,471 students were enrolled for advanced degrees in 884 reporting institutions. The *Directory of Music Faculties in Colleges and Universities, U.S. and Canada, 1970–1972* lists 14,500 faculty members (362 of whom teach in Canada) in 1,300 different colleges, universities, conservatories, schools of music, and community colleges.

VISUAL ARTS It is clearly true that the visual arts have moved onto the academic stage with no intention of leaving it (College Art Association of America, 1966). In spite of the evident excellence of many independent professional art schools, the idea of college is firmly implanted in the minds of many as the culminating reach of the educational process for artists. We do not, as in Germany, the Scandinavian countries, and other European nations, parallel university education with technical and crafts schools having equal (and substantial) state support. Our efforts instead reflect our individualistic attitudes toward education in the arts and echo our notions of free enterprise and variety in education generally. The first formal commitment to the education of artists (at institutional levels, as distinguished from goodness knows how many apprenticeship arrangements) was the school established as the Pennsylvania Academy of the Fine Arts in 1806. This school is still with us, still offering studio work without dependence on the degree credential our society weighs so heavily. Other schools followed: Maryland Institute (1826), the School of the Art Institute of Chicago, which preceded the museum (1866), Massachusetts College of Art (1873), the School of the Boston Museum of Fine Arts (1876), Cleveland Institute (1882), Kansas City Art Institute (1885), Minneapolis Art

NOTE: This section on visual arts is based on an unpublished manuscript by Norman L. Rice (1972), dean of the College of Fine Arts at Carnegie-Mellon University.

Institute (1886), Corcoran School of Art (1887), Brooklyn Museum Art School (1898), and John Herron School of Art (1902). All these were functioning early as studio centers for preparing painters and sculptors. But George Fisk Comfort at Syracuse in 1873 and John Ferguson Weir at Yale in 1869, along with the founders of art programs at the University of Illinois (1876) and a few other places, conceived practice in the arts as having humanistic values that were compatible with other, more literary, university pursuits. The invasion of the colleges by artists was an inevitable consequence, and art programs proliferated after 1900.

There was, in the beginning, no problem of separating the intentions of the independent professional schools from those of the colleges. The independent schools were looser in administrative organization and more flexible in their acceptance of students than the colleges could be. They were also less likely to infringe on the autonomy of studio professors. They remained indifferent to grades, credits, or final accolades. They were, in short, cast in the European atelier mold. The colleges, on the other hand, could not exempt a large class of students—art students—from the limitations imposed on the rest. They began to develop curricula that involved choices of activities and combinations of faculty members to match. Their scheduling and requirements formed an intricate network through which the student moved in accord with prevailing academic routines. Faculty members in the arts, in contrast with the part-time independent schoolteachers, reached for and gained all the rights, privileges, and perquisites (including tenure and committee assignments) of their fellow faculty members on campus. Artists in some numbers rejected the idea of regular employment as an erosion of their freedom to create in their own imagery. Others found the processes of eating regularly, working under institutional roofs, raising families with comparative security, and even, in a few places, occupying studios rent free a not too stultifying experience. The universities and colleges probably scrutinized the teaching capacities (though not necessarily the academic credentials) of an artist more closely than did their independent counterparts. Generally speaking, docile types tended to move toward the college studios, both as teachers and as students. More adventurous spirits, or those who could not for long tolerate any kind of prescription, continued to use the looser, more permissive, independent professional schools to gain whatever advantages they could from teachers with some reputation as artists and from association with free spirits of their own kind in an environment often enhanced (in the museum schools) by rich collections open for study and ready for exploitation by teachers and students alike.

In the 1930s a curious trend began. As a result of pressures developing in state departments of education aimed at making teacher certification requirements more rigorous, independent schools like the School of the Art Institute of Chicago, which had long had respectable teacher education programs in art, were nudged toward "improvement" of their credentials. Though credit from an unsanctioned professional school might have status among administrators locally, it could be rejected by school officials in the next state, for there was no "accredited" list of these schools. Professional art schools began the difficult process of moving into the charmed circle of the accredited schools (the colleges) through sporadic efforts to qualify for membership in the regional associations and thus gain inclusion on an acceptable "list." In Chicago it took two years of preparation and two reviews before the Art Institute's effort succeeded. The North Central Association did not admit another art school for 20 years at least. The Art Institute's pattern of development in its degree programs involved the addition of general humanities studies to its studio and art history core. These "academic" courses could be taken in any accredited schools, though most students found it convenient to use the University of Chicago's downtown college, which offered a generous range of late afternoon and evening classes. The B.F.A. was established as a respectable degree in this independent art school, and perhaps in others, to the benefit of teachers, state scholarship recipients, returning veterans with government educational benefits, rehabilitation students, and many more. Parents (who as a class tended to regard arts education with mistrust) were softened at the sight of a degree program in an art institute prospectus and overlooked the skylighted unorthodoxy of the cindery studios strung along the Illinois Central tracks.

To dwell on this transition from purely studio-centered instruction to a mixture of studio and general studies is only a way of emphasizing how effective the mixture became, how potent the combination of studio and classroom was, and of noting the relative promptness of colleges to develop the opportunity they now had within their reach. College-based programs in studio arts grew slowly before World War II but, nourished by the flow of returning veterans, they grew rapidly after the war both in numbers and in

academic importance. The colleges, indifferent, unaware, or be-
lieving the arts to be polite and amenable pursuits, patted the
camel's nose as it appeared inside the tent.

It has been suggested that there are other, more appropriate,
ligatures between the practice of art and the traditional academic
disciplines than the incorporation of studio courses into the family
of campus curricula. Generally, such speculations go back to something like the art institute pattern, but with degree-granting author-
ity moving toward the college partner and practice assigned as the
proper responsibility of a satellite institute or conservatory. Such
a division of labor obviously preserves the sanctity of scholarship
while allowing students to study the things they really want to
learn. There was perhaps once a moment in history when such
institutional arrangements could have become the rule rather than
the exception. It appears to be far too late now to go into reverse
on any very general scale. Practicing artists have found their way
into the patterns of academe without (as they have discovered)
losing their identity as professionals. They are firmly installed
on faculties. The visual arts they teach have accommodated themselves on the campus to the mechanical problems of scheduling,
grades, and credits that go along with college membership.

In the process of being assimilated, studio faculties have for-
feited in many cases their privilege of accepting and retaining for
studio instruction only students who show initial dedication and
continuing ability to perform well as independent problem solvers.
Among the compromises confronting studio teachers is trying to
come to terms with nonprofessional students—those who use art
as a means of satisfying curiosity, as recreational release, or as a
balance to heavy academic fare. In many cases the resulting programs have yielded excellent creative and educational fruit. The
humanities have embraced the arts as brothers—or at least cousins;
the arts have become naturalized even when they are not fully inte-
grated. The parallel phenomenon is worth noting. As art has gained
in academic respectability, as graduates have moved out of the colleges into the academic marketplace, the degree syndrome has in-
fluenced administrative judgments. Art faculty members are not
quite the free agents they once were; the degree credential, having
become more common, has been confused with artistic or teaching
competence. It is a case of the colleges succumbing to their own
propaganda: students have been guided toward degree programs,
have moved toward intellectualization; and art generally has pro-

duced a new generation of idea-oriented artists, capable of thinking art-as-object right out of existence. All this may have been inevitable in any case. But the independent or studio-based professional schools have responded to the challenge of campus-based artist–teachers by themselves moving toward the colleges in both intention and process.

The *American Art Directory* of the American Federation of Arts (1970) provides information on the scope and dimensions of art programs in the United States today. This directory lists professional art schools, colleges, and universities that offer a major in art; schools of architecture; and individual artists who conduct classes of professional standards. Data, including number of full-time and part-time faculty, degrees offered, majors enrolled, tuition costs, etc., are given for each listing. An extract from this list of college and university programs in the visual arts indicates 605 four-year institutions and 74 two-year institutions, or a total of 679 schools offering a major in art. (Schools of architecture are not included in these extracted numbers.) Full-time faculty number 7,275 in four-year schools and 433 in two-year schools, a total of 7,708. Part-time faculty number 2,934 in four-year schools and 185 in two-year schools, a total of 3,119. This is a total faculty of 10,827. Not all schools reported the number of majors enrolled, but 57,100 in four-year institutions and 4,855 in two-year institutions, or a total of 61,955, were indicated.[2] In addition to these numbers are the schools (often schools of museums) that offer courses in joint programs with a partner university, which is the degree-granting institution. Examples of this arrangement are the Corcoran School of Art/George Washington University and the Art Academy of Cincinnati/University of Cincinnati.

What the future holds is not easy to foresee. Art will survive, through the forms it takes, both as an educational enterprise and as each art in its own idiosyncratic development. These changes, perhaps radical, will be conditioned by the emergence of new social, technological, philosophical, and human opportunities. A good part of the changes will reflect the residual effect of art as a college-based educational enterprise. The colleges have the obligation as well as the opportunity to make the process work.

[2] Information on class enrollments of "students majoring in art and of others taking art courses" is provided, but the data are essentially impossible to interpret since some schools are obviously reporting their entire college enrollment without so indicating and others may be doing this also. In addition, it is not specified that these figures are for an academic year.

ART MUSEUMS A major descriptive study of museums in the United States, the first and only report of its kind, was made by the U.S. Office of Education (1969) in 1966. Of the 2,889 museums in the study, 303 are in colleges and universities and 166 of these are art museums or exhibit art in conjunction with historical and/or scientific displays. This means, roughly, that about 8 percent of the four-year colleges and universities in the United States have something that can be called an art museum. Seventy-nine percent of those 166 art museums have a paid staff, but only twenty-eight percent have a full-time paid staff. Twelve and one-half percent, or 37 institutions, have a professional paid staff of 25 or more. Forty-three percent have a paid staff of 10 or less. On operating expenditures, 42 percent of the institutions spend $5,000 or less per year. Ten institutions, or 3.3 percent, spend $250,000 or more per year, and three of those ten spend over $1 million per year. Sixteen percent carry on formal research. Thirty-six point seven percent, or 22 institutions, provide training for professional workers. The study identifies "quality indicators," and the art museums in colleges and universities receive high scores on qualities such as professionally designed exhibits, professional staff, and educational cultural activities.

Museums of all types are in a transitional stage in which they are seeking to identify their missions. (For example, is the museum a treasure house for the use of a scholarly elite or a regular part of the life of the ordinary citizen?) Museums in colleges and universities are no exception. Considering the expense of a really useful museum (the Smithsonian or the Los Angeles County, for example), can a university administration justify such an effort? Senseless duplication is foolish, especially in places like New York, where existing museums are already, in effect, an extension of the classroom for all colleges in the area. Still, scholars and painters want their own galleries and studios. In Iowa City or Omaha, on the other hand, the problem is not the same as in New York. In rural areas, the question of a permanent collection versus only traveling exhibits is a lively one. In a democratic society spread geographically from ocean to ocean, it is not enough that New York is the most complete and exciting city for the arts in the world. Are students in Fargo, North Dakota, and Jackson, Mississippi, to be limited to a diet of slides and reproductions of great works of art—on whatever scale they may be screened? And must they forgo the opportunity to study in a working museum? Must they forgo any "hands-on" experience? These serious questions are too often dismissed with oversimplified "practical" answers. They are problems with which the arts must deal.

ARCHI-TECTURE In 1814 Thomas Jefferson proposed, for the first time in any country, that a professional curriculum in architecture be incorporated into a university program. This proposal was not developed in the University of Virginia, however, and only one course in the history and principles of classic architecture—which lasted only until the Civil War—materialized.

Essentially, before the Civil War, the few practitioners of architecture in the United States who had any professional training had gotten it in Europe; the only means of getting into practice in the United States was to apprentice in the office of one of the existing architects. During the first half of the nineteenth century some of the technical problems relevant to the concerns of architecture were studied in isolated classes in such places as the Military Academy at West Point (1802); the University of Virginia, where civil engineering courses began in 1826; Harvard's Lawrence Scientific School (1847); Yale's School of Engineering; the University of Michigan (in the science curriculum); and Rensselaer Polytechnic Institute.

Architecture itself, however, was not established in American higher education until the Massachusetts Institute of Technology decided in 1865 to establish a professional course in the discipline and appointed William Robert Ware to plan and head this new curriculum (Weatherhead, 1941). Ware was a Boston architect who, after graduating from Harvard College, had studied in the New York atelier of Richard Morris Hunt, who had attended the Ecole des Beaux Arts in Paris and had enthusiastically brought back to the United States the principles and spirit of that institution. For two years after his appointment by MIT, Ware observed architectural training in London and Paris and made plans for the first American school. His courses opened in 1868 with four students. The program prospered and by 1875 there were 32 students.

The actual establishment of MIT (though the charter had been granted a few years earlier) was effected through the Morrill Land Grant Act of 1862. The next two architecture programs were also formed in land-grant universities. Cornell established a professional course of architectural study in 1871 as a part of its College of Engineering, which was thereafter known as the College of Engineering and Architecture. The University of Illinois provided for a full professional course in 1867 and brought it to fruition in 1873. Then Syracuse installed architecture and painting as the two original departments in its College of Fine Arts, which was established in 1873. Five more schools followed before the end of the century:

- Columbia University

- The University of Pennsylvania

- George Washington University (then called Columbian University)

- The Armour Institute of Technology (now Illinois Institute of Technology), in cooperation with the Art Institute of Chicago, which provided the drawing and design component

- Harvard University

Of the architecture programs in these nine original schools, two were connected with fine arts divisions and seven were officially departments of engineering. The total enrollment in 1898 was 384 regular and 124 special students. By 1930, 53 schools, with a total enrollment of 4,575 were offering a full professional course in architecture.

The American Institute of Architects (AIA) was founded in 1857 to raise the standards of the profession. It immediately established a committee on education in which a great deal of discussion took place in the following years on curricula and policies. In 1912, through informal discussion at an AIA convention, the idea of an Association of Collegiate Schools of Architecture (ACSA) developed. That organization was founded in the same year to stimulate contacts between the schools and to establish informal educational standards through control of admission to its membership. In 1914 ACSA established "standard minima," but these were abandoned in 1932. In 1939 the National Architectural Accrediting Board (NAAB) was established to study programs at various institutions and to publish an annual list of approved schools. The board was specifically denied any power to standardize schools and was instructed to evaluate each program in its own terms.

It is not surprising that, when the impetus to establish professional architectural training in the United States developed, these programs were set up within universities, since it was the American tradition to center advanced training of almost any kind in these institutions. No doubt, these programs were usually assigned to engineering on the basis of a mutual interest in materials and building. Most architecture departments, however, found that being a subdivision of engineering was constrictive to the development of a well-balanced program in architecture and struggled to become independent units.

In the early years of the twentieth century a compelling interest in design, often somewhat divorced from problems of construction and economics, developed in architecture on the campus. There was a burst of enthusiasm for the Ecole des Beaux Arts. American students went to Paris to study, and Frenchmen were imported to run the design programs in American universities. An American alumni society of Beaux Arts students was established which offered design competitions that became so popular that they practically dominated the methods and objectives of design teaching throughout the country.

From the very beginning, then, architecture in higher education was faced with the problem of integrating the various components of the discipline into a balanced and meaningful program of instruction and professional practice. It is by its very nature a field that involves a wide spectrum of concerns and interests.

Architecture participated fully in the population expansion and growth in higher education during the twentieth century, experiencing the characteristic drop-off in growth and enrollment during the Depression. Today the ACSA, whose membership includes all degree programs in architecture, lists 87 full members in the United States. In their brochure, *1971/1972 Enrollments and Statistics,* they report a total enrollment for 78 reporting schools (64 of which are accredited by NAAB) of 23,569 full-time students and 1,509 part-time students. The faculty for these schools is composed of 1,336 full-time and 1,033 part-time members, or a total full-time equivalent faculty of 1,687. During the past few years, approximately one new school has been added to the ACSA each year, and this growth rate is expected to continue. The U.S. Office of Education (1970) reports in *Earned Degrees Conferred* that in 1969–70 the following degrees were granted in architecture: 3,902 bachelor's degrees, 658 master's degrees, and 11 doctor's degrees. Not included in either of these sets of figures are the many courses taken by students not enrolled in a degree program.

Perhaps of all the arts in higher education today, architecture faces some of the most difficult problems. Integrating diverse components is an inherent problem for architecture, but the specialized concerns of the present are almost staggering in range and complexity: all aspects of planning; economics, especially banking; political science, not to mention politics; sociology; aesthetic and emotional needs; ecology; and, of course, engineering. The acuteness of the problems besetting our cities and the confusion engendered by rapid and often erratic changes make the architect's task even more perplexing.

Eero Saarinen expressed the idea that an architect always designs with the next larger context in mind, and some have extended this idea by saying that there are no architects today, only architect-planners. This direction of thinking, which relates a given structure to the nearest watershed as well as to the street it is on, brings the architectural problem to environmental design, a concept now guiding many schools. In any case, the social, economic, technical, and aesthetic aspects of architecture are currently subject to violent change, and both the complexity and the extreme flux in the field are frustrating to those who are seeking to manage its problems. (Consider, for example, the problems Saigon and its needs present today for the architect-planner.) It is crucial, in such circumstances, that the aesthetic component of architecture be strengthened to contribute as vitally as possible to this effort. This is not a call for the architect to return to the era of the Parthenon or even of Sir Christopher Wren, but the conviction that, however the field develops, the aesthetic should be a strong component of the architectural-planning mix.

FINE ARTS CENTERS Building complexes for the arts, usually called fine arts centers, have been growing in number since campus building programs burgeoned after World War II. Two institutions in this study, Earlham College and Dartmouth College, are fine examples of schools which have arts centers that were designed and built to be an integral part of campus life. John Sloan Dickey, former president of Dartmouth, was deeply involved in the development of Hopkins Center and was largely responsible for the placement of the campus post office and all student mailboxes in the middle of this fine arts complex. This arrangement brings students, throughout their daily activities, within the physical environs in which artists are working, and in which galleries and concert halls are located.[3] Runyan Center at Earlham is a combination student center and fine arts center. A current prob-

---

[3] The Henry Art Gallery at the University of Washington in Seattle was once on the edge of the campus and was usually one of the most deserted places there. When the campus building program established a new center of campus life in its proximity, the gallery began to teem with people.

lem in many schools, however, is the need to bring work done at the arts center into the curricular life of the university. Also, just as scientists would not want their laboratories preempted by visiting colleagues, neither should artist-teachers have their own spaces turned over to visiting artists.

The idea of bringing the physical plant for the arts into the day-to-day life of the campus, often through combinations with other activities in readily accessible areas, is a sound one. A special study of the nature and effectiveness of such physical centers for the arts is long overdue and would provide much useful knowledge for future planning.

THE CONCERT SERIES Campuses have had "concert series" of some kind, including the Chautauqua, since the Civil War, but the development of campus presentations since World War II has been virtually spectacular. Campus bookings, fees, and gross have been page-one headline stories in *Variety,* the show business trade paper. The Association of

TABLE 1
Program type comparison

	Symphony	Vocal recital	Instrumental recital	Chamber music
Percentage of gross fees	15	4	7	5
Average fee (dollars)	5,036	2,111	1,468	1,149
Gross attendance (percent)	71	57	64	64
Student attendance (percent)	42	32	41	36
Average performances per campus	2.33	1.80	3.11	3.11
Total performances	159	94	246	237
Availability (percentage of schools programming at least one of the events)	38	29	45	43
Auditoriums Performance halls over 1,000 (percent)	70	53	52	37
Performance halls under 1,000 (percent)	12	37	35	57
Field houses (percent)	15			
Lecture halls (percent)				

SOURCE: Association of College and University Concert Managers, 1970.

College and University Concert Managers (ACUCM) started surveying its field in 1965 and provided a standard form and report beginning in 1970, when it had 360 colleges and universities in active membership. The 133 institutions reporting in 1970 spent $5,250,000 for various events in the 1969–70 concert season. The types of programs presented at these 133 institutions in 1970 and their comparative characteristics are indicated in Table 1, which appeared in the ACUCM survey.

The impact of these programs with off-campus talent — especially in places more than one hour's driving time away from Boston, New York, Chicago, Los Angeles, and San Francisco — is extremely important but remains virtually unstudied. An important development over the last five years or so has been the closer involvement of these programs with the academic departments in the arts. Faculty on cultural affairs committees, for example, have been able to relate events, programming, and artists to course work on an increasing number of occasions. More important, however, is the prac-

Theater	Dramatic readings	Ballet	Contemporary dance	Jazz	Rock	Folk	Popular	Opera and choral
21	1	6	5	2	14	3	14	2
3,174	1,037	3,216	2,083	1,894	6,031	1,130	4,647	4,970
67	56	71	60	68	72	55	69	66
48	46	44	50	57	72	55	58	42
4.90	1.78	2.04	2.32	1.45	3.70	3.02	4.17	1.63
353	50	96	123	61	126	133	163	18
41	16	27	30	24	19	25	22	6
61	41	72	56	55	51	60	56	80
30	33	15	33	33		23	18	10
					36		18	
	15							

tice of retaining the artists on the campus before or after the concerts for master-classes, seminars, and informal discussions. More study is needed to phase the artist into curricular and extracurricular campus life. The Artists in the Schools program of the National Endowment for the Arts in the Public Schools (K–12) may well be worth the attention of arts administrators on the campus.

3. National Statistical Studies

National statistics on various levels and in various fields of study in American higher education have been gathered and published by the National Center for Educational Statistics of HEW's Office of Education and by the Office of Research of the American Council on Education. Specific information on the arts can be extracted from these figures. Compilations of statistics relating to the arts in higher education taken from the studies indicated are included in the following appendixes of this report:

- Appendix B   *Earned Degrees Conferred, 1967–68, 1968–69, 1969–70,* U.S. Office of Education, National Center for Educational Statistics

- Appendix C   *Digest of Educational Statistics, 1970,* U.S. Office of Education, National Center for Educational Statistics

- Appendix D   *The American Freshman: National Norms for Fall 1971, National Norms for Entering College Freshmen—Fall 1966–Fall 1970,* American Council on Education, Office of Research

- Appendix E   *The American Graduate Student: A Normative Description,* American Council on Education, Office of Research, 1971

Growth is generally indicated in all these data. Specifically, the number of bachelor's degrees conferred in fine and applied arts rose from 25,555 in 1967–68 to 35,945 in 1969–70; master's degrees, from 6,563 to 7,849; and doctor's degrees, from 528 to 734. Bachelor's degrees in architecture rose from 2,956 to 3,902 during the same period. It is interesting to note in the data that the growth rate for bachelor's degrees in art (listed as arts general under fine and applied arts) conferred during this period was 49 percent, while bachelor's degrees in art education grew only 23 percent. The most dramatic and long-reaching change to observe, however, in the difference between the occupations of freshmen's fathers and the students' own major and career plans. In 1971 only .8 percent of freshmen surveyed reported that their fathers were artists, yet 9 percent of these same students planned to major in the arts and 6 percent (teachers excluded) intended to try to make a living as artists.

More sophisticated statistical analysis of data available on the arts from national studies would be welcome to the field. A considerable contribution to the clarity and usefulness of these data to the arts has recently been made by the National Center for Educational Statistics itself. It has developed a new, greatly improved, taxonomy for the arts, which was first used in survey forms in 1970–71 and will extend over at least the next five years without change. This new classification system at last groups the arts on the basis of common goals and discipline. It does away with the illogical and outdated combination of speech and dramatic arts, moving speech out of fine and applied arts altogether. Further, it separates the critical and creative branches of art and music—though surprisingly does not extend this crucial distinction to the other arts. It also subdivides the former large category under fine and applied arts, "all other fields." This new taxonomy for the arts is as follows (National Center for Educational Statistics, 1970*b*, p. 8):

1000 FINE AND APPLIED ARTS
      Subject field designations which characterize students, faculty, facilities, degree programs, research projects, etc., having to do with the creation and appreciation of the diverse modes of communicating ideas and emotions by means of stylized, visual and non-visual representations.

1001 Fine arts, general

1002 Art (painting, drawing, sculpture)

1003 Art history and appreciation

1004 Music (performing, composition, theory)

1005 Music (liberal arts program)

1006 Music history and appreciation (musicology)

1007 Dramatic arts

1008 Dance

1009 Applied design (ceramics, weaving, textile design, fashion design, jewelry, metalsmithing, interior decoration, commercial art)

1010 Cinematography

1011 Photography

1099 Other, specify

It will be very helpful when the national statistical figures on the arts no longer include figures for speech, and when the above important internal discriminations within the arts can be made. Until this reordering is achieved in published materials, it is necessary to bear in mind the shortcomings of existing and past classifications.

Professor Noah M. Meltz of the Institute for the Quantitative Analysis of Social and Economic Policy at the University of Toronto has done some in-depth statistical studies based on published and unpublished statistics of the National Center for Educational Statistics (NCES). He has derived patterns in degrees granted since 1950–51 in both the United States and Canada and has developed projections to 1980–81 with the assistance of the Office of Education, among others. His studies break down degrees into the various fields of study, but problems of taxonomy raise their heads. For comparative purposes, Meltz regrouped the data from the National Center for Educational Statistics to correspond to the categories used in Canada by the Dominion Bureau of Statistics. Thus, he separated music out of fine arts, but left speech and dramatic arts and all other fields of study in the arts within the fine arts category. He also placed education graduates with field specialties rather than with education, as is the case in the NCES 1970 publication, *Earned Degrees Conferred*. This means that art education is included in fine arts, and music education is included in music, groupings quite congenial to the present study. But since speech and dramatic arts was an existing NCES category and since Meltz was consistent in his treatment of education, he included "Education: Speech and Hearing Impaired" in his fine arts category. That degrees granted for speech therapy could be grouped with degrees in the arts is a dramatic indicator of the need for the new taxonomy of the arts which the National Center for Educational Statistics has developed.[1]

Three tables from Meltz on bachelor's and first professional degrees follow. Table 2 shows growth patterns in fields of study from 1951 to 1969 in terms of both numerical and percentage distributions. Among the fields of study are architecture, fine arts (including art education, speech and dramatic arts and their education components, and all other fields in the arts except music), and music (including music education). Table 3 shows projections to 1981 in

---

[1] To be sure, Meltz recognized this need and said, "A more in-depth probing of the composition of fields of study would be extremely valuable."

TABLE 2 *Bachelors and first professional degrees granted in the United States in total numerical and percentage distribution for 1951, 1960, and 1969*

	Numerical distribution			Percentage distribution		
	1951	*1960*	*1969*	*1951*	*1960*	*1969*
Total graduations	386,266	391,194	769,222	100.00	100.00	100.00
Natural science and related				30.42	29.33	22.61
Agriculture, engineering, and forestry	53,638	45,163	52,456	13.89	11.55	6.82
Health professions	23,678	24,450	33,498	6.13	6.25	4.35
Science	40,155	45,090	88,036	10.40	11.53	11.44
Social sciences, humanities, and related				69.58	70.67	77.37
Architecture	2,644	1,801	3,477	0.68	0.46	0.45
Arts (Letters)	89,080	92,264	258,870	23.06	23.59	33.65
Education	65,038	71,145	121,669	16.84	18.19	15.82
Fine arts	9,890	12,887	35,024	2.56	3.29	4.55
Law	14,338	9,240	17,468	3.71	2.36	2.27
Music	7,723	7,593	12,107	2.00	1.94	1.57
Social work	2,951	2,498	8,404	0.76	0.64	1.09
Other	77,131	79,063	138,213	19.98	20.22	17.97

NOTE: Percentages may not add to 100 because of rounding.
SOURCE: Meltz, 1971a, p. 19.

terms of numerical distributions, and Table 4 shows projections to 1981 in terms of percentage distributions. In his projections, Meltz (1971a, p. 102) offers two alternative estimates for 1981. "Estimate A is based on the assumption that the percentage distribution of males and females separately in each year is the same as occurred in 1968–69. . . . Estimate B is based on extrapolating trends during the 1960's in the percentage distribution of the total." These tables show a growth in fine arts from 2.56 percent of all graduations in 1951 to 4.55 percent in 1969—a growth of 80 percent. The growth projected to 1981 is less marked in both Estimate A and Estimate B.

On April 17, 1972, the *Chronicle of Higher Education* (p. 1) reported the projections of the National Center for Educational Statistics for 1980–81 from tables that have not yet been published. These data indicate that enrollments in public colleges and universities will increase by about 70 percent in the next decade, while enrollments in private institutions will increase by about 8 percent.

TABLE 3
Alternative projections of the distribution of total bachelor's graduations by field of study in the United States in 1981 and actual data for 1961 and 1969

	Actual		Estimated in 1981	
	1961	*1969*	*A*	*B*
Total graduations	397,383	769,222	1,170,080	1,170,080
Natural science and related				
Agriculture, engineering and forestry	42,431	52,456	73,480	59,680
Health professions	24,634	33,498	51,568	42,330
Science	46,563	88,036	130,184	140,310
Social sciences, humanities, and related				
Architecture	1,674	3,477	4,903	5,580
Arts (Letters)	97,645	258,870	396,940	529,535
Education	74,028	121,669	197,792	108,870
Fine arts	12,861	35,024	55,564	64,740
Law	9,429	17,468	24,620	23,780
Music	7,360	12,107	18,958	8,830
Social work	2,718	8,404	13,400	23,240
Other	78,040	138,213	202,671	163,185

SOURCE: Meltz, 1971*b*, p. 21.

TABLE 4
Alternative projections of the percentage distribution of bachelor's graduations by field of study in the United States in 1981 and actual data for 1961 and 1969

	Actual		Estimated in 1981	
	1961	*1969*	*A*	*B*
Total graduations	100.00	100.00	100.00	100.00
Natural sciences and related				
Agriculture, engineering, and forestry	10.68	6.82	6.28	5.10
Health professions	6.20	4.35	4.41	3.62
Science	11.72	11.44	11.13	11.99
Social sciences, humanities, and related				
Architecture	0.42	0.45	0.42	0.48
Arts (Letters)	24.57	33.57	33.92	45.26
Education	18.63	15.82	16.90	9.30
Fine arts	3.24	4.55	4.75	5.53
Law	2.37	2.27	2.10	2.03
Music	1.85	1.57	1.62	0.75
Social work	0.68	1.09	1.15	1.99
Other	18.93	17.72	17.10	13.04

NOTE: Percentages may not add to 100 because of rounding.
SOURCE: Meltz, 1971*b*, p. 20.

The growth in earned degrees is projected as follows:

	1970–71 (Estimated)	1980–81 (Estimated)
Bachelor's and first professional	863,000	1,333,000
Natural sciences	188,860	257,200
Social sciences, humanities	674,140	1,075,800
Fine arts	59,710	98,650
Master's	224,000	395,900
Natural sciences	44,060	70,860
Social sciences, humanities	179,940	325,040
Fine arts	14,210	25,060
Doctor's	32,000	68,700
Natural sciences	14,650	26,060
Social sciences, humanities	17,350	42,640
Fine arts	1,120	2,660

In these figures, bachelor's degrees in fine arts are projected to increase by 66 percent, master's by 76 percent, and doctorates by 138 percent. These increases, it should be noted, are in data on students earning degrees rather than on class enrollments—a critical factor in the growth of the arts. Indications are that while the number of majors in the arts will experience normal growth in line with the general increase in higher education population, class enrollments in the arts will go up at an even higher rate.

4. Profiles of Selected Colleges and Universities

The information on each institution included in this study was gathered by means of a questionnaire (see Appendix F) which was, of course, subject to limitations. The nomenclature in the arts varies widely (a taxonomy for classifying institutions in the field has not yet been invented) and records—under various guises—have only recently begun to appear. Accordingly, *the arts* has been little understood as an entity in higher education. What is included under this designation is almost a local option. In one institution the arts means (visual) arts and music, while in another the term might include cosmetology and regional planning and omit art history.

The questionnaire used in this study listed areas in the arts as architecture, dance, film, music, theater, (poetic) writing, and visual arts (as well as "other," to allow for local options). This definition of the arts, which certainly would include the crafts, deliberately drops the word "fine" (as too precious for this day and age); it makes an effort to preserve the meaning of the word "arts," and to prevent its misuse as "the arts and sciences" or as shorthand for liberal arts. Confusion here could be minimized by substituting "letters" for "arts." At present it is not clear countrywide whether *fine arts* means the classic grouping of painting, sculpture, and ceramics, or all the arts, or simply art history alone. Further, the current metamorphosis in architecture, as it strives to incorporate in its program elements of planning, sociology, political science, economics (particularly banking), as well as engineering, highlights what all the arts are going through as they leave an elitist or "conspicuous waste" position for a guttier position at the center of society and its schools. Emerging new relationships, some subtle and some not so subtle, are expressed in ideas such as "easel painting is dead," in earth art, and in the interpenetration of the arts (e.g., mixed media, comparative arts, and aesthetic education). But even when an art takes on political, social, and/or economic components, as architecture and some street theater have done, the aesthetic component still exists and is the binding factor in giving the arts a common relationship in the operational sense.

The intent here is to give a comprehensive view of the concept of the arts for those interested in higher education, not to provide a "definitive study" or handbook for operating the arts on campus. Although programs of diverse natures on various campuses could not all be met with a neat fit by the same questionnaire, the cooperating institutions—gallantly, for the most part—accepted the intent of the questionnaire and responded in extremely effective ways.

Selecting the schools to include in the study was a difficult task. After many abortive efforts to invent a neat classification for a small number of institutions offering the arts (small enough to be feasible for this study) which would recognize such factors as size, location (extremely important for the availability of professional performances, distinguished museums, and lively galleries), style, comprehensiveness, control (public or private), etc., I simply chose those which in my own judgment provided diversity and interest. At least a half-dozen other institutions could have been used for each of those selected and included here, but limitations of time and money prevented the use of them all. Nor is there any implication that the institutions selected are national examples from any point of view other than that of representing contrasts and comparisons among many kinds of programs in the arts. Later studies will undoubtedly provide suitable classifications for wider and deeper investigations—particularly for the community college, a much neglected portion of higher education that will enroll half the freshmen of the country by 1975.

The results given here, then, represent a reconnaissance or gathering of information for a preliminary statement on the dimensions of the arts in academe and do not represent one school of thought or "best" way. On the other hand, despite great variations in definitions, practices, records keeping, and accounting methods, the results do give some bench marks useful for orientation to the recent growth in the arts.[1] Identification and assessment of academic

---

[1] Figures for specific programs and ranges are, I believe, more useful than averages. Since numbers have to be related to programs to be fully meaningful, the scope of actual individual programs is more informative than computed averages. A study that I did in 1971 for the International Council of Fine Arts Deans (based on information supplied by 56 of the 91 members)

programs in terms of educational principles, quality of teaching, quality of student and faculty work, and other criteria of this type are not attempted, but critical information is provided for the educator and the layman concerned about the arts specific to given institutions whose programs may be studied. Although the information provided by the schools varies greatly in reliability and may reflect biases or distortions in the perceptions of the individual reporters, those interested in starting or expanding programs can, nevertheless, identify some parameters related to specific programs which can be used in planning or assessment.

reported annual budgets for colleges or other administrative units of the arts (i.e., two or more departments) ranging from $13,402 to $5,818,586; total student majors from 54 to 2,391; and capital investment in buildings from $1,078 to $9,500,000. Computing averages for budgets or capital investment from these data would be utterly meaningless.

The Washington-Baltimore campus of Antioch College is an experimental wing, only three years old, of a progressive college. Among many interesting aspects of current innovation on that campus is the promising effort of using the arts resources of the Washington-Baltimore complex as a "college without walls." With their advisers, students work out a curriculum involving museums, art schools, dance groups, other colleges and universities, theaters, film centers, other campuses of the college (Yellow Springs and San Francisco), and formal classes at the campus headquarters.

To promote student interest and awareness, the arts program is advertised in various underground student newspapers; but recruitment, as well as all the other problems of admissions, is something which this campus still must work out. Nevertheless, the student body is growing modestly and, after some internal administrative strife in 1971–72, the trustees have renewed their interest in the arts program.

Perhaps the most significant aspect of this program is its basic interest in contributing to the artistic life of the surrounding communities, as well as drawing on them as teaching resources. This puts into practice, at least on an experimental level, the idea of serving the urban community, as university extension centers served the rural, agricultural community in the last third of the last century and the first half of this one.[2]

The arts at the Washington-Baltimore campus are administered by a director of the arts program. He has a relatively free hand in developing the program and, with faculty and students, prepares his annual budget (approximately $135,000 for fiscal 1973) which he presents to the dean of the campus. At this point, there exists a policy difficulty which recently has been somewhat clarified in favor of the director of the arts program. The director describes this development as a "struggle on this Antioch campus between the social scientists' (heavy leftists) concept of arts as nonverbal com-

---

[2] The new Boston campus of the University of Massachusetts (College III), under the statewide presidency of Robert C. Wood, is working to develop a program along these lines. The President's Committee on the Future University of Massachusetts, chaired by Vernon R. Alden and composed of laymen, faculty, and students, has clearly opened the way for such developments. It is likely that College III will pursue a direct, meaningful relationship with all quarters of the Boston community when it opens in 1973.

munication devices for adding feelings to information versus the arts' perception of the arts as in themselves change agents. This has led to what now appears to be a loss of self-governance for the arts. It appears as if they'll be service activities supporting social science programs and supplying degree requirements in the humanities area."

All this suggests the sort of problems campuses face as they become more involved with the community; in this context, the arts can hardly be regarded any longer as one of the frills of higher education. As part of the leading edge for change in our society, the arts are presented with interesting and serious problems. Their worst mistake would be to walk away from these challenges.

ANTIOCH COLLEGE, WASHINGTON-BALTIMORE CAMPUS

Administration

1. Year institution of higher education founded: This campus, 1969.

2. Subjects in the arts first offered.

Film	1969
Writing	1969
Photography	1969
Music	1970
Theater	1970
Visual arts	1970
Video	1970

3. Arts program established in 1970. Chief officer is called the director. He reports to the dean of the campus.

4. Present administrative structure is due to: powerful personality and careful design.

Student Personnel

1. Numbers of majors enrolled in the arts were:

Undergraduates	1971	1970	1969
Film			3
Music	4	2	
Theater	7	9	
Writing	15	10	5
Visual arts	1	4	
Video	12	7	
Photography	10	7	2
TOTAL	49	39	10

No graduate students

2. Total numbers of class enrollments of all students (nonmajors and majors) in all classes in the fall term were:

Undergraduates	1971	1970
Film	45	25
Music	27	17
Theater	25	12
Writing	100	60
Visual arts	3	10
Video	35	15
Photography	57	22
TOTAL	292	161

No graduate students

Faculty Personnel

	Number of full-time faculty FTE	Number of part-time faculty (bodies)	Sum of all FTE's	Number of student teaching assistants
Dance				1
Film		2	0.75	1
Music		1	0.67	
Theater	1	3	2.75	5
Writing	1	3	2.00	1
Video		1	0.80	2
Photography	1	2	2.00	1
TOTAL	3	12	8.97	11

NOTE: Antioch reports student majors and class enrollments in visual arts for 1970 and 1971, but no faculty members in this area at the present time. The explanation for this is that in 1970 and 1971 visual arts students were taught by a part-time faculty member (shared with another institution) who is no longer with the college. Antioch now has arrangements with the Maryland Institute College of Art whereby Antioch students can take courses there on a tuition-free basis (and vice versa).

Budget, 1970–71

	Amount of budget	Percentage for salaries	Percentage for operating expenses
Dance	$ 500	100	0
Film	8,000	50	50
Music	4,000	50	50
Theater	15,000	85	15
Writing	15,000	98	2
Visual arts	5,000		
Video	16,000	50	50
Photography	16,000	85	15
TOTAL	$79,500	83	17
Administrative and general expenses of arts program	37,500		
TOTAL	$117,000		

Space and Equipment

1. The capital investment in buildings for the sum of the departments in the arts is:

    Zero. All space is rented.

2. The number of square feet for specialized studio and laboratory use (other than general classroom space) is:

Film	(Storage)
Music	750
Theater	5,600
Writing	625
Video	1,300
Photography	750
TOTAL	9,025 +

3. *a.* Renovated square feet needed:
        8,200 sq. ft.
   b. Additional square feet needed:
        5,000 sq. ft.

4. Capital investment for special equipment is:

Film	$ 750
Music	350
Theater	1,000
Writing	450
Video	5,000
Photography	1,000
TOTAL	$8,550

5. Projected costs of equipment needed for optimum operation are:

Film	$10,000
Music	15,000
Theater	12,500
Writing	2,000
Visual arts	3,000
Video	15,000
Photography	5,000
TOTAL	$62,500

Scholarships

The following undergraduate scholarships are awarded annually:

	Number	Total amount in dollars
Dance	1	$ 2,000
Music	1	2,000
Theater	6	14,000
Writing	2	6,000
Video	2	5,000
Photography	1	2,000
TOTAL	13	$31,000

NOTE: These are all college work/study program jobs.

Qualitative Considerations

1. *a.* Is creative work considered equivalent to research in other disciplines as a criterion for promotion?
    Yes.
   b. Is an advanced academic degree required for appointment to the regular faculty?
    No.

2. Is there a growing question of the efficacy of tenure for faculty in the arts in your college?
    No tenure on this campus.

3. Effectiveness of departments (faculty) in the following areas is felt to be:
   a. Contribution of new works in performance and exhibits: moderately
   b. Development of an increasing sophisticated laity (audience):   moderately
   c. Exploration of contemporary trends (arts movements):   very effective
   d. Vital, stimulating exploration of the heritage of each of the arts to introduce the seminal forces of the past: not enough
   e. Seeking new relationships in the arts: moderately

4. Do you feel your college is having any appreciable effect on the content and procedures of education in the arts in the schools –kindergarten through twelfth grade—in your state?
    No. Just beginning theater and music for public schools. Four months into a reform school program in creative writing.

5. Admission for undergraduates in the arts is determined by:
   Campus admissions office in haphazard relation to arts program.

6. A student major may be dropped from the college or department because:
   He drops out himself as a result of not being involved in projects.

7. Impact on the surrounding community by student and faculty artists is felt to be:
   Medium. It is very early in the development of the program.

8. Are you satisfied with your contribution to the number of "successful" working artists?
   Faculty: No.   Student: No.

Arts Events

1. Are you provided with funds in the budget over and above any box office returns to produce arts events?
   Yes.

   The budgets for this purpose annually amount to:

Film	$3,700
Writing	500
TOTAL	$4,200

2. Are the arts directly involved in the cultural events presented by off-campus artists:
   a. By having ex officio members on the "cultural presentations" committee?
   Not answered.
   b. By directly relating these events to curricular work?

Dance	Yes
Film	Yes
Music	Yes
Theater	Yes
Writing	Yes
Visual arts	Yes
Video	Yes
Photography	Yes

3. Total number of arts events (all arts) from off-campus for which tickets are sold:

   None. All events (including film showings) are free.

   Total admissions to arts events from off-campus: 4,300

   Total income from arts events from off-campus: $2,100

   Total expenses for arts events from off-campus: $6,000

4. Estimates of the percentage breakdown of attendance between *(a)* students and faculty and *(b)* the community at major on-campus events of the following type are:

	Student/Faculty (percent)	*Community (percent)*
Dance	40	60
Film	90	10
Music	20	80
Theater	20	80
Writing	30	70
Visual arts	50	50
Video	30	70
Photography	50	50

Founded in 1925, Bennington College introduced divisions of dance, drama, music, and visual arts seven years later and has stuck with these divisions ever since. The arts have always been central to the curriculum here, and Bennington has produced individuals and programs which have made distinct contributions to the arts, particularly in dance. Between 1969 and 1972, "interdivisional majors," which combine the arts, increased from four to twenty-two. Although Bennington is subject to the same pressures that all small private colleges are experiencing these days, such as finance, admissions, and demand for specialities, it still demonstrates how effective a small college can be when it provides a focus on the arts in its curricular efforts.

Note that in all the divisional budgets, no more than 86 percent (82 percent in visual arts, 81 percent in theater, 66 percent in interdivisional) goes for salaries; the remainder covers operating expenses (production, equipment, materials, etc.). This percentage for salaries is low compared to English departments, for example, where salaries usually account for over 95 percent of the budget. Sometimes the lower percentages spent on salaries in the arts and the sciences are held against these fields by faculty in the humanities, as counter to their own efforts for higher salaries. But the frame of reference for such an argument is misleading. If history and English departments were charged their fair share of the cost of library acquisitions and operations, their higher percentages for salaries would drop noticeably. In the arts and the sciences, laboratory materials and space are a necessary added expense, and salary costs are not appropriately used if laboratory expenses aren't in suitable proportion. Any department in the arts which spends much more than 85 percent on salaries is probably shortchanging its faculty and students.

BENNINGTON COLLEGE

Administration

1. Year institution of higher education founded: 1925.

2. Divisions in the arts formed:

Dance	1932
Music	1932
Theater	1932
Visual arts	1932

3. No separate administrative unit for the arts.

4. Present administrative structure is due to: careful design.

Student Personnel

1. Numbers of majors enrolled in the arts were:

Undergraduates	*1971*	*1970*	*1969*
Dunce	18	17	13
Music	16	19	11
Theater	18	18	5
Visual arts	29	38	29
*Interdivisional**	22	13	4
TOTAL	103	105	62

Graduates	*1971*	*1970*	*1969*
Dance		1	1
Theater	2		1
Visual arts	2	2	2
TOTAL	4	3	4

*Interdivisional combines the arts.

2. Total numbers of class enrollments of all students (nonmajors and majors) in all classes in the fall term were:

Undergraduates	*1971*	*1970*	*1969*	*1968*	*1967*	*1966*
Dance	147	144	102	69	59	
Music	343	238	215	130	88	
Theater	162	186	121	147	85	
Visual arts	321	376	349	260	273	
Interdivisional		44				
Black music	111	64				
Photography	33	21				
TOTAL	1,117	1,073	787	606	505	

Graduates	1971	1970	1969	1968	1967	1966
Dance		2				
Music	2	1	1			
Theater			1	4	5	2
Visual arts	6	7		5	8	
Architecture				1		
Dance for Drama						1
Design for dance			3			
Design for drama				3		
TOTAL	8	10	5	13	13	3

Faculty Personnel

	Number of full-time faculty FTE	Number of part-time faculty (bodies)	Sum of all FTEs	Number of student teaching assistants
Dance	3	4	5.25	5
Music	7	2	8.50	3
Theater	3	1	3.50	3
Visual arts	6	2	7.00	2
Interdivisional		*	0.50	
TOTAL	19	9	24.75	13

* Varies.

Budget, 1970–71

	Amount of budget	Percentage for salaries	Percentage for operating expenses
Dance	$ 71,932	86	14
Music	138,267	86	14
Theater	70,282	81	19
Visual arts	110,307	82	18
Interdivisional	11,900	66	34
TOTAL	$402,688		

Space and Equipment

1. The capital investment in buildings for the sum of the departments in the arts is $1,400,000.

2. The number of square feet for specialized studio and laboratory use (other than general classroom space) is:

Dance	3,545
Music	5,290
Theater	1,778
Visual arts	22,393
TOTAL	33,006

3. Additional square feet needed:
   107,850

4. Capital investment for special equipment is:
   Not answered.

5. Projected costs of equipment needed for optimum operation are:
   Estimates not available.

Scholarships

The following undergraduate scholarships are awarded annually:

	Number	*Total amount in dollars*
Dance	3	$14,850

Qualitative Considerations

1. *a.* Is creative work considered equivalent to research in other disciplines as a criterion for promotion?
      Yes.
   b. Is an advanced academic degree required for appointment to the regular faculty?
      No.

2. Is there a growing question of the efficacy of tenure for faculty in the arts in your college?
      No.

3. Effectiveness of departments (faculty) in the following areas is felt to be:
   a. Contribution of new works in performance and exhibits: very effective

b. Development of an increasingly sophisticated laity (audience): very effective
c. Exploration of contemporary trends (arts movements): very effective
d. Vital, stimulating exploration of the heritage of each of the arts to introduce the seminal forces of the past: moderately
e. Seeking new relationships in the arts: very effective

4. Do you feel your college is having any appreciable effect on the content and procedures of education in the arts in the schools—kindergarten through twelfth grade—in your state?
   No. No college or school of education.

5. Admission for undergraduates in the arts is determined:
   By the college.

6. A student major may be dropped from the divisions:
   Because of lack of talent and/or performance without necessarily referring to grades.

7. Admission to graduate work is made:
   With auditions and/or portfolio.

8. Impact on the surrounding community by student and faculty artists is felt to be:
   Medium.

9. Are you satisfied with your contribution to the number of "successful" working artists?
   Faculty: Yes.   Student: No.

Arts Events

1. Are you provided with funds in the budget over and above any box office returns to produce arts events?
   Yes.

The budgets for this purpose annually amount to:

College	$ 5,000
Dance	1,000
Music	3,000
Theater	750
Visual arts	4,500
TOTAL	$14,250

2. Are the arts directly involved in the cultural events presented by off-campus artists:

   a. By having ex officio members on the "cultural presentations" committee?

      Not answered.

   b. By directly relating these events to curricular work?

      Yes for all departments.

3. Total number of arts events (all arts) from off-campus for which tickets are sold:

      None. No charge for events.

   Total expenses for arts events from off-campus: $2,500

4. Estimates of the percentage breakdown of attendance between *(a)* students and faculty and *(b)* the community at major on-campus events of the following type are:

	Student/Faculty (percent)	*Community (percent)*
Dance	95	5
Music	75	25
Theater	85	15
Visual arts	95	5

The college of Fine Arts at Carnegie Institute of Technology (now Carnegie-Mellon University) was founded in 1905. One of the first comprehensive colleges of fine arts in the country, it includes all the arts, although writing is shared with the English department. Architecture and visual arts were the first majors, both offered in 1905. Music was added in 1913 and theater (which now includes film and dance), in 1914. The college has been highly respected in the arts since its founding. It was an architect, Henry Hornbostel, who convinced Andrew Carnegie that the institution should attempt to be strong in the arts. Enrollments have been stabilized mainly because of space. A dean of the college reports to the vice-president of academic affairs. The college is firmly ensconced in the university, with well-earned respect campuswide for the new disciplines in the arts. The budget is prepared by the dean in consultation with the department heads and presented to the vice-president of academic affairs.

Carnegie-Mellon is one of the few reasonably successful models of a professional undergraduate college in the arts. The college controls its admissions by having each department set its own criteria and requires portfolios and/or auditions and interviews. Any student not making satisfactory progress may be dropped at any time. There is good support for undergraduate scholarships. A key to Carnegie-Mellon's success is its primary emphasis on achievement in specialization.

CARNEGIE-MELLON UNIVERSITY

Administrative

1. Year institution of higher education founded: 1900.

2. Departments in the arts formed:

Architecture	1905
Visual arts	1905
Music	1913
Theater	1914

3. College of Fine Arts established in 1905. Chief officer is the dean, who reports to the vice-president of academic affairs.

4. Present administrative structure is due to: powerful personality was influential.

Student Personnel

Numbers of majors enrolled in the arts were:

Undergraduate	1971	1970	1969	1968	1967	1966
Architecture	160	158	178	161	163	180
Music	164	147	155	147	156	164
Theater*	184	179	191	183	170	181
Painting and sculpture	177	190	201	197	205	284
Design	150	143	147	140	135	55†
	835	817	872	828	829	864

Graduate	1971	1970	1969	1968	1967	1966
Architecture	18	18	9	5	17	16
Music	41	34	38	42	32	32
Theater*	51	43	30	33	31	37
Painting and sculpture	24	18	18	11	8	7
Design	3	4	5	2	0	0
TOTAL	137	117	109	93	88	92

*Includes dance, film, and TV.

† The 1966 undergraduate figure for design (55) was the enrollment in the department of graphic arts, which merged with industrial design to form the present department of design.

NOTE: The figures given here for majors are a body count of students enrolled in the classes of each department. These figures provide a picture of the number of majors since only a very few nonmajors—either from outside the College of Fine Arts or from other departments within the college—are enrolled in classes. Also for this reason, actual class enrollments totals were not reported. The college also provides elementary arts instruction at general education levels, but no figures are available.

Faculty Personnel

	Number of full-time faculty FTE	Number of part-time faculty (bodies)	Number of student teaching assistants
Architecture	22	8	
Music	21	14	1
Theater	23	3	
Painting and sculpture	22	2	3
Design	11	0	
TOTAL	99	29	4

Budget, 1970–71

	Amount of budget	Percentage for salaries	Percentage for operating expenses
Architecture	$ 320,406	94.7	5.3
Music	392,130	88.9	11.1
Theater	439,593	90.2	9.8
Painting and sculpture	326,677	96.0	4.0
Design	169,888	92.7	7.3
Sum of departments	$1,648,694		
Dean's office	73,360	62.8	37.2
TOTAL	$1,722,054	90.9	9.1

Space and Equipment

1. The capital investment in buildings for the College of Fine Arts is:
   Not answered.

2. The number of square feet for specialized studio and laboratory use (other than general classroom space) is:

Architecture	12,125+
Music	10,242
Theater	7,989+
Painting and sculpture	25,254
Design	10,783
TOTAL	66,393+

3. Additional square feet needed:
   A new teaching theater has been approved, and construction should begin this spring. Until plans for this building are completed, it is difficult to say in detail how much more space is needed, though all departments do need more space.

4. Capital investment for special equipment is:
   Data not available.

5. Projected costs of equipment needed for optimum operation are:
   Visual arts is the only area that has prepared a careful estimate. Needs: $45,612.
   Rough estimate of the needs of the college: $750,000.

Scholarships

The following undergraduate scholarships and graduate fellowships, teaching and otherwise, are awarded annually:

	Number of undergraduate scholarships	Total amount in dollars	Number of graduate fellowships	Total amount in dollars
Architecture	81	$ 75,264	5	$ 18,000
Music	132	120,692	12	7,692
Theater	131	164,083	20	81,830
Painting and sculpture	119	117,112	25	29,900
Design	82	80,142	1	4,000
TOTAL	545	$547,293	69	$141,422

Qualitative Considerations

1. *a.* Is creative work considered equivalent to research in other disciplines as a criterion for promotion?
    Yes.
   b. Is an advanced academic degree required for appointment to the regular faculty?
    No.

2. Is there a growing question of the efficacy of tenure for faculty in the arts in your college?
    Yes. This question is being widely discussed here as elsewhere.

3. Effectiveness of departments (faculty) in the following areas is felt to be:
   a. Contribution of new works in performance and exhibits: moderately to very effective
   b. Development of an increasingly sophisticated laity (audience): moderately
   c. Exploration of contemporary trends (arts movements):   very effective in theater, painting/sculpture, design, and architecture; moderately in music
   d. Vital, stimulating exploration of the heritage of each of the arts to introduce the seminal forces of the past: very effective in theater, painting/sculpture, design, and architecture; moderately in music
   e. Seeking new relationships in the arts: very effective, but difficult in this school, where specialized preoccupations are strong

4. Do you feel your college is having any appreciable effect on the content and procedures of education in the arts in the schools—kindergarten through twelfth grade—in your state?

> Yes. The education programs (in painting/sculpture and music) are small, but in the dean's judgment are highly effective.

5. Admission for undergraduates in the arts is determined:

> By the university admissions in consultation with the college. (Only students acceptable to the departments are admitted.) With auditions and/or portfolio.

6. A student major may be dropped from the college or department:

> Because of lack of talent and/or performance without necessarily referring to grades.

7. Admission to graduate work is made:

> By the departments of the college, with overall control vested in a grade committee of the college, and with auditions and/or portfolio.

8. Impact on the surrounding community by student and faculty artists is felt to be:

> Medium to strong. More could be done, if more exhibition, performance, and lecture space were available.

9. Are you satisfied with your contribution to the number of "successful" working artists?

> Faculty: Yes.   Student: Yes.

Arts Events

1. Are you provided with funds in the budget over and above any box office returns to produce arts events?

> The college does not have any box office events.

2. Are the arts directly involved in the cultural events presented by off-campus artists by having ex officio members on the "cultural presentations" committee?

> No.

3. Total number of arts events (all arts) from off-campus for which tickets are sold:

> None.

4. Estimates of the percentage breakdown of attendance between *(a)* students and faculty and *(b)* the community at major on-campus events of the following type are:

	Student/Faculty (percent)	*Community (percent)*
Theater	50	50

NOTE: No way to estimate numbers in other areas.

Dartmouth's deliberate program to make the arts more central to the college appears to be working. My observation is that it's working better than most by a considerable margin. By design, philosophically and architecturally. Hopkins Center is a focus for student, faculty, and community activity; it has involved many individuals in the crafts as well as in arts events presented both by students and faculty and by professional artists from off campus. (There may be more film buffs per dormitory here than anywhere else in the world.) The relationship of the Hopkins art complex to the academic program is enhanced by an interesting administrative arrangement in which the director of the Hopkins Center has responsibilities in the academic program. Thus there is a deliberate bond between the work of the center and the departments of music, theater, and the visual arts. (The academic programs for dance and film are in the drama department. Dartmouth was an early significant contributor to the growth of the student film maker in the United States.)

Dartmouth is a fine example of an institution whose administration, students, and faculty have coordinated their efforts to make the arts integral to campus life, both socially and academically. Officials are quick to point out that their objectives are far from being reached—they express disappointment in the lack of penetration into the community and surrounding schools and the unevenness of the various arts. However, an outsider can only admire the developments in the arts on this campus over the years. Interestingly enough, these developments paralleled the general rise of the arts across the country: the arts were entirely extracurricular before the turn of the century; individual courses were introduced around 1900; a department of music was established in the twenties; and then came two departments, a building, and strong administrative support in the sixties. The seventies should be interesting for the arts at Dartmouth.

DARTMOUTH COLLEGE

Administration

1. Year institution of higher education founded: 1769.

2. Departments in the arts formed:

Music	1923
Art	1928
Theater	1968

3. No separate administrative unit for the arts.

4. Present administrative structure is due to: tradition, historical chance, powerful personality, and careful design.

Student Personnel

1. Numbers of majors enrolled in the arts were:

Undergraduates	1971	1970	1969
Art*	32	48	46
Music	12	10	13
Theater	12	9	10
TOTAL	56	67	69

No graduate students

* Figures here include majors in visual studies (major established in 1969) and majors in art history, two programs which are combined in the department of art at Dartmouth. Breakdowns into these two components are given in other data.

2. Total numbers of class enrollments of all students (nonmajors and majors) in the fall term were:

Undergraduates	1971	1970	1969	1968	1967	1966
Art history	287	297	283	258	212	268
Visual studies	124	143	101	111	81	105
Music*	204	205	50	83	106	109
Theater	84	102	112	93	33	66
Architecture	100	104	83	23	12	16
Dance	14	22	27			
Film †	15	23	61			
Writing	49	38	43	38	45	68
TOTAL	877	934	760	606	489	632

No graduate students

† The class enrollment figures for film courses are somewhat misleading, since almost all courses in film are taught in the winter and spring terms.

* Total music class enrollments are up largely as a result of the introduction of courses related to jazz and improvisational music.

NOTE: Class enrollment figures have been given for the following subjects which are not actually departments: architecture (in visual studies), dance and film (in theater), and writing (in the department of English).

Faculty Personnel

	Number of full-time faculty FTE	Number of part-time faculty (bodies)	Sum of all FTE's
Art history	5	4	5.67
Visual studies	5	1	5.33
Music	7	2	7.80
Theater	7		7.00
Architecture		1	.30
Dance	1	1	1.25
Film		3	.80
TOTAL	25	12	28.15

Budget, 1970–71

	Amount of budget	Percentage for salaries	Percentage for operating expenses
Art history	$ 86,680		
Visual studies	114,910	82	18
Music	300,800	55	45
Theater	197,100	68	32
TOTAL	$699,490		

NOTE: If the amounts spent for galleries, crafts workshops, summer arts festivals, and administrative costs of the Hopkins Center were added, the total budget would be between $1,000,000 and $1,100,000.

Space and Equipment

1. The capital investment in buildings for departments in the arts is:

Music	$ 947,700
Theater	2,276,100
Visual studies	900,100
TOTAL	$4,123,900

NOTE: Does not include Hopkins Center.

2. The number of square feet for specialized studio and laboratory use (other than general classroom space) is:

Music	11,350
Theater	31,602
Visual studies	15,600
TOTAL	58,552

3. *a.* Renovated square feet needed:
8,300

   b. Additional square feet needed:
10,000

4. Capital investment for special equipment is:

Music	$ 80,000
Theater	125,000
Visual studies	30,000
TOTAL	$235,000

5. Projected costs of equipment needed for optimum operation are:

Music	$ 30,000
Theater	50,000
Visual studies	20,000
TOTAL	$100,000

Scholarships

No undergraduate scholarships are assigned by discipline, and there is no graduate work in the arts.

Qualitative Considerations

1. *a.* Is creative work considered equivalent to research in other disciplines as a criterion for promotion?
Yes.

   b. Is an advanced academic degree required for appointment to the regular faculty?
No.

2. Is there a growing question of the efficacy of tenure for faculty in the arts?
Yes.

3. Effectiveness of the departments (faculty) in the following areas is felt to be:
   a. Contribution of new works in performance and exhibits: moderately to very effective. Varies from year to year and from department to department.
   b. Development of an increasingly sophisticated laity (audience): not answered.
   c. Exploration of contemporary trends (arts movements): moderately. Led by visual studies program, dance, and one or two people in music.
   d. Vital, stimulating exploration of the heritage of each of the arts to introduce the seminal forces of the past: very effective in art and theater, moderately in music.
   e. Seeking new relationships in the arts: not enough. Little formal interdepartmental endeavor.

4. Do you feel your program is having any appreciable effect on the content and procedures of education in the arts in the schools—kindergarten through twelfth grade—in your state?
   > Yes. Mainly as a result of their coming to us (the Hopkins Center), not as much as there should be as a result of our going to them— but this is developing.

5. Admission for undergraduates in the arts is made:
   > By Dartmouth College admissions. The departments are not generally involved until majors are chosen.

6. A student major may be dropped from the departments:
   > Because of grades below a certain point.

7. Impact on the surrounding community by student and faculty artists is felt to be:
   > Strong. Our homegrown musical and theatrical events have a strong direct impact on local residents, less impact on schools, lesser still on business and industry.

8. Are you satisfied* with your contribution to the number of "successful" working artists?
   > Faculty: No.   Student: No.

* One is never satisfied, but in theater and visual studies many recent graduates have done well. In film (even without a department) Dartmouth has made a significant contribution for many years, commensurate with its size and character.

Arts Events

1. Are you provided with funds in the budget over and above any box office returns to produce arts events?
   Yes.

   The budgets for this purpose annually amount to:

Music	$ 50,000
Theater	80,000
TOTAL	$130,000

2. Are the departments directly involved in the cultural events presented by off-campus artists:
   a. By having ex officio members on the "cultural presentations" committee?
   No.
   b. By directly relating these events to curricular work?
   Not answered.

3. Total number of arts events (all arts) from off-campus for which tickets are sold:
   Approximately 60.

   Total admissions to arts events from off-campus: approximately 34,000

   Total income from arts events from off-campus: $86,000

   Total expenses for arts events from off-campus: $92,500

4. Estimates of the percentage breakdown of attendance between *(a)* students and faculty and *(b)* the community at major on-campus events of the following type are:

	Student/Faculty *(percent)*	*Community* *(percent)*
Film	70	30
Music—Pop	95	5
Music – Classical	50	50
Theater	40	60
Visual arts	50	50

DUKE UNIVERSITY

As far as the arts are concerned, Duke looks today like many colleges and universities did 40 or 50 years ago. The only departments, art and music, were housed for many years in an old barnlike fire hazard on the very edge of the women's campus, behind the gym. Theater is combined with speech in the English department, and dance is a part of physical education. The arts have little contact with each other. Creative work is not considered equivalent to scholarly research in other fields.

But perhaps things are changing. With support from national private foundations the music department has demonstrated what could be done in both academic and professional areas of the curriculum. Ground has been broken on a new $2.5 million building for music. The department is sponsored to send out performing artists, and there is a resident string quartet. The small dance program in the women's division of the physical education department is coming into its own—only two years ago male students were allowed for the first time to take dance for credit. The program has grown from 79 class enrollments in the fall of 1969 to 224 in 1971. Duke has had a small creative writing program in the English department for some years. Several students from this program have published novels that rated national acclaim. One of these students is now a writer-in-residence at Duke. The visual arts department is in a state of flux at the present time but plans further development in art history. The department has grown in majors, though not in class enrollments, since a graduation requirement which was satisfied by the introductory art history course was dropped in 1969.

DUKE UNIVERSITY

Administration

1. Year institution of higher education founded: 1839 (Trinity College).

2. Departments in the arts formed:

Visual arts	1932
Music	1953

3. No separate administrative unit for the arts.

4. Present administrative structure due to: tradition.

Student Personnel

1. Numbers of majors enrolled in the arts were:

Undergraduates	1971	1970	1969
Music	40	35	00
Visual arts	47	31	28
TOTAL	87	66	60

No graduate students

2. Total numbers of class enrollments of all students (nonmajors and majors) in all classes in the fall term were:

Undergraduates	1971	1970	1969	1968	1967	1966
Music*	392‡	420	408	386	372	
Visual arts*	301	382	406	471	527	434
Dance†	224	126	79	69	49	56
TOTAL	917	928	893	926	948	490

No graduate students

* In both art and music, a general introductory course in history and appreciation fulfilled a graduation requirement until 1969 when this requirement was dropped.

† Dance is included in the department of health and physical education.

‡ The lower figure for music class enrollments for 1971 reflects the fact that several faculty members were on leave and fewer courses were offered.

NOTE: Creative writing courses and theater courses exist in the English department.

Faculty Personnel

	Number of full-time faculty FTE	Number of part-time faculty (bodies)
Music	15	
Visual arts	10	6
Dance	2	
Writing		2
TOTAL	27	8

Budget, 1970–71

	Amount of budget	Percentage for salaries	Percentage for operating expenses
Music	$216,881	90.0	10.0
Visual arts	*	*	*
Dance	22,462	97.2†	2.5†
TOTAL	$239,343		

* Not answered.

† Percentages do not total 100 because of rounding.

Space and Equipment

1. The capital investment in buildings for departments in the arts is:
     Figures not given for existing buildings. $2.5 million building for music under construction.

2. The number of square feet for specialized studio and laboratory use (other than general classroom space) is:

Music	56,000
Visual arts	1,600
Dance	6,300
TOTAL	63,900

3. Is the present plant effective for current artistic endeavor?
     No.   Specific needs for space not stated.

4. Capital investment for special equipment is:
     Not answered.

5. Projected costs of equipment needed for optimum operation are:
     Not answered.

Scholarships

The following undergraduate scholarships are awarded annually:

	Number	Total amount in dollars
Music	10	$10,000

Qualitative Considerations

1. *a.* Is creative work considered equivalent to research in other disciplines as a criterion for promotion?

    No.

    b. Is an advanced academic degree required for appointment to the regular faculty?

    Yes, or equivalent in recognition and experience.

2. Is there a growing question of the efficacy of tenure for faculty in the arts?

    No. Possible in the future.

3. Effectiveness of the departments (faculty) in the following areas is felt to be:

    a. Contribution of new works in performance and exhibits: very effective in visual arts (considering the small size of the faculty); moderately in music

    b. Development of an increasingly sophisticated laity (audience): moderately in music

    c. Exploration of contemporary trends (arts movements): moderately in music

    d. Vital, stimulating exploration of the heritage of each of the arts to introduce the seminal forces of the past: moderately in music

    e. Seeking new relationships in the arts: moderately in music and in visual arts

4. Do you feel your program is having any appreciable effect on the content and procedures of education in the arts in the schools — kindergarten through twelfth grade — in your state?

    No. There is little interest in the arts by school administrators.

5. Admission for undergraduates in the arts is made:

    By the departments after admission to the university, and with auditions in music.

6. A student major may be dropped from the departments:

    In music, because of lack of talent and/or performance or because of grades below a certain level. In visual arts, because of grades below a certain level.

7. Impact on the surrounding community by student and faculty artists is felt to be:

    Strong in music. Weak in visual arts.

8. Are you satisfied with your contribution to the number of "successful" working artists?

> Music: Faculty: Not answered   Student: Yes
> Visual Arts: As a nonprofessional school, this lies outside the immediate objectives.

Arts Events

1. Are you provided with funds in the budget over and above any box office returns to produce arts events?

> Music: Yes

The budget for this purpose annually amounts to:

> $5,000 (music).

2. Are the departments directly involved in the cultural events presented by off-campus artists:

   a. By having ex officio members on the "cultural presentations" committee?

Music	Yes
Visual arts	No

   b. By directly relating these events to curricular work?

Music	Yes
Visual arts	No

3. Total number of arts events (all arts) from off-campus for which tickets are sold:

> Response unclear.

4. Estimates of the percentage breakdown of attendance between *(a)* students and faculty and *(b)* the community at major on-campus events of the following types are:

	Student/Faculty *(percent)*	*Community* *(percent)*
Music	75	25
Visual arts	85	15

EARLHAM COLLEGE   Earlham College is the epitome of the small liberal arts college— in this case, a sectarian school of Quaker origin which is still a Quaker-style operation. There is a fine arts office for the three departments with a secretary but no head, chairman, director, or dean. There is a convener who calls the group together on rare occasions, less than once a year. The departments have chairmen who work closely together. Both tradition and design keep the administration in this pattern. Close working relationships with other members of the faculty are apparent in college meetings, which are often of great length, since they seek consensus on all college matters. At one point when a new arts complex was delayed, a chemist renounced all funds for his department until the arts complex (Runyan Center) was in the works.

Class enrollments in the three departments increased from 466 to 686 between the fall semester of 1966 and that of 1971; but it is difficult to assess growth patterns in majors because the arts are often included in interdepartmental majors such as art and biology, drama and literature, and art and psychology. The number of students majoring strictly in the arts has decreased since 1969, but the college reports that the number of interdepartmental majors, including one of the arts, is increasing.

EARLHAM COLLEGE

Administration

1. Year institution of higher education founded: 1847.

2. Departments in the arts formed:

Visual arts	1883
Music	1885
Theater	1910

3. No separate administrative unit for the arts.

4. Present administrative structure is due to: tradition and careful design.

Student Personnel

1. Numbers of majors enrolled in the arts were:

Undergraduates	1971	1970	1969
Music	2	3	3
Theater (speech/drama)	†	†	1
Fine arts*	4	7	8
TOTAL	6	10	12

No graduate students

* The fine arts major is an interdepartmental major within the arts.

† Not answered.

NOTE: Figures are not included for interdepartmental majors which include non-arts departments. Such combination majors as biology and art, psychology and art, and literature and drama are popular and are reported to be increasing.

2. The total numbers of class enrollments of all students (nonmajors and majors) in all classes were:

Undergraduates	Fall term only 1971	Entire year 1970	1969	1968	1967	Fall term only 1966
Music	215	261	214	258	279	199
Theater	194	212	286	284	279	145
Visual arts	123	294	268	371	211	122
Fine arts	154					
TOTAL	686	767	768	913	769	466

No graduate students

Faculty Personnel

	Number of full-time faculty FTE	Number of part-time faculty (bodies)	Sum of all FTEs
Music	3	8	3.98
Theater	2	1	2.50
Visual arts	3	2	3.70
TOTAL	8	11	10.18

NOTE: There are no teaching assistants.

Budget, 1970–71

	Amount of budget	Percentage for salaries	Percentage for operating expenses
Film	$ 28,963	69	31
Music	59,851	88	12
Theater	26,621	96	4
Visual arts	47,242	86	14
Fine arts	7,427	71	29
TOTAL	$170,104	87	13

Space and Equipment

1. The capital investment in buildings for the sum of the departments in the arts is:

    Approximately $1,347,052. The departments in the arts and the Student Center share a building which cost $2,694,104. Approximately 50 percent of the building is used for the arts. It is not possible to allocate by various departments.

2. The number of square feet for specialized studio and laboratory use (other than general classroom space) is:

Dance	2,000
Music	15,000
Theater	20,000
Visual arts	5,000
TOTAL	42,000

3. Is the present plant effective for current artistic endeavor?

    Yes.

4. Capital investment for special equipment is:

    None spent in these areas for 1970–71.

5. Projected costs of equipment needed for optimum operation are:

Music	$150,000
Theater	1,000
Visual arts	10,000
TOTAL	$161,000

Scholarships

The following undergraduate scholarships are awarded annually:

	Number	Total amount in dollars
Music	1	$400

Qualitative Considerations

1. *a.* Is creative work considered equivalent to research in other disciplines as a criterion for promotion?
   Yes.
   b. Is an advanced academic degree required for appointment to the regular faculty?
   No.

2. Is there a growing question of the efficacy of tenure for faculty in the arts in your college?
   No more so than with other faculty.

3. Effectiveness of departments (faculty) in the following areas is felt to be:
   a. Contribution of new works in performance and exhibits: very effective
   b. Development of an increasingly sophisticated laity (audience): very effective
   c. Exploration of contemporary trends (arts movements): very effective
   d. Vital, stimulating exploration of the heritage of each of the arts to introduce the seminal forces of the past: very effective
   e. Seeking new relationships in the arts: very effective

4. Do you feel your college is having any appreciable effect on the content and procedures of education in the arts in the schools—kindergarten through twelfth grade—in your state?
   No. No art education program.

5. Admission for undergraduates in the arts is determined by:
   The college admissions office.

6. A student major may be dropped from the college or department:
   Because of evaluation below a certain point or because of below-normal progress in the number of courses successfully completed in relation to the number of terms in attendance.

7. Impact on the surrounding community by student and faculty artists is felt to be:

Music	Strong
Theater	Medium
Visual arts	Medium

8. Are you satisfied with your contribution to the number of "successful" working artists?

    Faculty: Yes.   Student: Yes.

Arts Events

1. Are you provided with funds in the budget over and above any box office returns to produce arts events?

    Yes.

    The budgets for this purpose annually amount to:

    $26,500 for film, music, and theater.

2. Are the departments directly involved in the cultural events presented by off-campus artists:

    a. By having ex officio members on the "cultural presentations" committee?

    Yes.

    b. By directly relating these events to curricular work?

Music	Yes
Theater	Yes
Visual arts	Yes

3. Total number of arts events (all arts) from off-campus for which tickets are sold:

    Approximately seven a year.

    Total admissions to arts events from off-campus: Circa 900

    Total income from arts events from off-campus: $800 or $900

    Total expenses for arts events from off-campus: $9,000

**FISK
UNIVERSITY** In 1972, Fisk created a new administrative structure, a Division of the Arts. Although still in need of space, faculty, and financial support (in equipment alone, the division estimates its current needs at $750,000), the new division is on its way to being central in the work of the university and has strong administrative support. A fine arts center is planned, new interdisciplinary programs are underway, and new programs for teacher training and new public school approaches have been designed. The chairman of the new division reports for all the arts to the dean of the university. The developments in the arts at Fisk and the way its leaders are coming to grips with the problems they face may well provide an example of change for other predominately black colleges in the South, as well as other schools.

FISK UNIVERSITY

Administration

1. Year institution of higher education founded: 1866.

2. Departments in the arts formed:

Music	1871
Writing	1920
Visual arts	1931
Dance	1952
Film	1968

3. Division of the Arts established in 1972. Chairman of the division reports for all the arts to the dean of the university.

4. Present administrative structure is due to: careful design.

Student Personnel

1. Numbers of majors enrolled in the arts were:

NOTE: J. Edward Atkinson compiled and edited *Black Dimensions in Contemporary American Art* (1971), with an introduction by Professor David C. Driskell of Fisk University. This book discusses 50 selected black painters with illustrations of their work. It may be significant for administrators in higher education to note that 43 of the 50 began their careers in colleges or universities.

Undergraduates	1971	1970	1969
Dance	13	10	10
Film	7	5	5
Music	55	45	40
Theater	40	35	25
Writing	10	15	25
Visual arts	45	35	25
TOTAL	170	145	130

Graduates	1971	1969
Music	5	2

2. Total numbers of class enrollments of all students (nonmajors and majors) in all classes in the fall term were:

Undergraduates	1971	1970	1969	1968	1967	1966
Dance	95	80	70	56	40	36
Film	7	5	5	5		
Music	450	370	350	345	330	320
Theater	300	250	125	120	100	100
Writing	10	15	25	75	75	75
Visual arts	450	410	370	350	340	300
TOTAL	1,312	1,130	945	951	885	831

Graduates	1971	1970
Music	5	2

NOTE: Writer-in-residence left the university in 1968.

Faculty Personnel

	Number of full-time faculty FTE	Number of part-time faculty (bodies)	Number of student teaching assistants
Dance	1		
Film		1	1
Music	10	2	
Writing	1		
Visual arts	5	2	
TOTAL	17	5	1

Budget, 1970–71

	Amount of budget	*Percentage for salaries*	*Percentage for operating expenses*
Dance	$ 13,000	90	10
Film	3,000	90	10
Music	120,000	75	25
Theater	50,000	75	25
Writing	5,000	90	10
Visual arts	85,000	70	30
TOTAL	$276,000	75	25

Space and Equipment

1. The capital investment in buildings for the arts is:

Music	$120,000
Theater*	50,000
Visual arts†	130,000
TOTAL	$300,000

* Includes dance.
† Includes film.
NOTE: Writing is included in English.

2. The number of square feet for specialized studio and laboratory use (other than general classroom space) is:

Music	2,000
Theater	1,000
Visual arts	7,000
TOTAL	10,000

3. Additional square feet needed:
   50,000 (includes an auditorium)

4. Capital investment for special equipment is:

Music	$150,000
Theater	25,000
Visual arts	50,000
TOTAL	$225,000

5. Projected costs of equipment needed for optimum operation are:

Dance	$ 25,000
Film	25,000
Music	300,000
Theater	200,000
Writing	25,000
Visual arts	200,000
TOTAL	$775,000

Scholarships

The following undergraduate scholarships and graduate fellowships, teaching and otherwise, are awarded annually:

	Number of undergraduate scholarships	Total amount in dollars	Number of graduate fellowships	Total amount in dollars
Music	5	$5,000	2	$6,000
Visual arts	3	3,000		
TOTAL	8	$8,000	2	$6,000

Qualitative Considerations

1. *a.* Is creative work considered equivalent to research in other disciplines as a criterion for promotion?
   Yes.
   b. Is an advanced academic degree required for appointment to the regular faculty?
   No.

2. Is there a growing question of the efficacy of tenure for faculty in the arts in your university?
   No.

3. Effectiveness of departments (faculty) in the following areas is felt to be:
   a. Contribution of new works in performance and exhibits: very effective
   b. Development of an increasingly sophisticated laity (audience): moderately
   c. Exploration of contemporary trends (arts movements): very effective

    d. Vital, stimulating exploration of the heritage of each of the arts to introduce the seminal forces of the past: very effective

    e. Seeking new relationships in the arts: very effective

4. Do you feel your college is having any appreciable effect on the content and procedures of education in the arts in the schools—kindergarten through twelfth grade—in your state?

    Yes. New programs are designed for use in the schools.

5. Admission for undergraduates in the arts is determined:

    By the university admissions in consultation with the departments.

6. A student major may be dropped from the departments:

    Because of lack of talent and/or performance, or because of grades below a certain point.

7. Admission to graduate work is made:

    By the university with recommendations from the departments.

8. Impact on the surrounding community by student and faculty artists is felt to be:

    Strong. For many years Fisk University had to provide the entire Nashville community with cultural events, and none were available from any other agent or university in the city. Later a symphony and art guild were founded. The university still provides the major cultural events for the entire North Nashville population of 38 percent of the city's residents.

9. Are you satisfied with your contribution to the number of "successful" working artists?

    Faculty: No.   Student: No.

Arts Events

1. Are you provided with funds in the budget over and above any box office returns to produce arts events?

    Yes.

  The budgets for this purpose annually amount to:

    Data not available.

2. Are the arts directly involved in the cultural events presented by off-campus artists:

    a. By having ex officio members on the "cultural presentations" committee?

    Yes.

b.   By directly relating these events to curricular work?
Yes for all departments.

3.   Total number of arts events (all arts) from off-campus for which tickets are sold:
None, no events have admission charges.

4.   Estimates of the percentage breakdown of attendance between *(a)* students and faculty and *(b)* the community at major on-campus events of the following type are:

	Student/Faculty (percent)	Community (percent)
Dance	50	50
Film	90	10
Music	50	50
Theater	75	25
Writing	98	2
Visual arts	50	50

Harvard University, the first university in the United States, dating
from 1636, formally introduced departments in the arts about the
same time as the arts were being introduced in higher education in
other parts of the country: fine arts in 1874, music in 1890, architecture in 1895, and visual studies in 1968. This suggests that
the rise of the arts was more a function of society-at-large than a
result of careful thought and planning on the part of the universities. At present the most characteristic aspect of the arts at Harvard
is the curricular emphasis on the critical and theoretical and the
extracurricular emphasis on action in the studio and in performance. The diverse and decentralized nature of the university,
especially as seen in student activities in clubs and houses, is
wondrous to behold. Among many groups concerned with performance is the Harvard Friends of Blue Grass Music. Hopefully these
student-oriented arts activities will continue, and reports indicate
that fresh winds of change are mounting in the curricular area.
For example, "A Survey of the Arts at Harvard," completed in
January 1972 for consideration by a review committee, and the
interest of the new president in the arts are offered as evidence
that some new approaches to the arts may be developing.

The Fogg Museum, among other facilities on campus, has been
a training ground for curators of the first order for years, and
recently the new Carpenter Center has provided many opportunities for students in the visual arts and in other areas, particularly
film.

It is interesting that Harvard and Duke are the only two respon-
dents in this study that reported that creative work of the faculty
in the arts is not considered equivalent to research in science, social
science, and the humanities.

HARVARD UNIVERSITY

Administration

1. Year institution of higher education founded: 1636.

2. Departments in the arts formed:

Fine arts	1874
Music	1890
Architecture	1895
Visual studies	1968

3. No separate administrative unit for the arts.

4. Present administrative structure due to: historical chance.

Student Personnel

1. Numbers of majors enrolled in the arts were:

Undergraduates	1971	1970	1969
Music	49	49	39
Visual studies	85	83	91
TOTAL	134	132	130
Graduates	1971	1970	1969
Architecture	163	178	154
Music*	47	46	45
TOTAL	210	224	199

*Some of the graduate students in music are abroad.

NOTE: Harvard did not report information on its department of fine arts, which is separate from its department of visual and environmental studies.

2. Total numbers of class enrollments of all students (nonmajors and majors) in all classes in the fall term were:

Undergraduates	1971	1970	1969	1968	1967	1966
Music	521	438	508	552	458	460
Visual studies	815	619	579	521	127	122
Theater	64	50	40	40	40	38
Writing	95	76	87	88	90	95
TOTAL	1,495	1,183	1,214	1,201	715	715
Graduates	1971	1970	1969	1968	1967	1966
Architecture	727	*	*	*	*	*
Music	112	114	123	122	126	11
Visual studies	62	69	70	17	11	9
Writing	8	8	6	2	6	5
TOTAL	909	191	199	141	143	25

*Figures unknown.

Faculty Personnel

	Number of full-time faculty FTE	Number of part-time faculty (bodies)	Number of student teaching assistants
Architecture	18.5		
Music	12.0	1	
Theater	2.0		
Visual studies	25.0	3	16
Writing	6.0	4	
TOTAL	63.5	8	16

NOTE: The Harvard catalog lists 27 faculty members in the department of fine arts.

Budget, 1970–71

	Amount of budget
Architecture	$ 375,000
Music	404,000
Theater	198,000
Visual studies	528,000
TOTAL	$1,505,000

NOTE: Percentage breakdowns for salaries and operating expenses not available.

Space and Equipment

1. The capital investment in buildings for departments in the arts is:
   Data not available.

2. The number of square feet for specialized studio and laboratory use (other than general classroom space) is:

Architecture	21,000
Music	61,069
Visual studies	59,952
TOTAL	142,021

3. Is the present plant effective for current artistic endeavor?
   The need does exist for studio space in the undergraduate halls and for places to perform chamber music.

4. Capital investment for special equipment is:
   Data not available.

5. Projected costs of equipment needed for optimum operation are:
    Not answered.

Scholarships

There are only general undergraduate scholarships. None are for specific fields.

The following graduate fellowships, teaching and otherwise, are awarded annually:

	Number	*Total amount in dollars*
Architecture	136	$125,000
Music	37	85,000
TOTAL	173	$210,000

Qualitative Considerations

1. *a.* Is creative work considered equivalent to research in other disciplines as a criterion for promotion?
        No.
    b. Is an advanced academic degree required for appointment to the regular faculty?
        Ph.D. is required, with exceptions for equivalent standing.

2. Is there a growing question of the efficacy of tenure for faculty in the arts?
        No.

3. Effectiveness of the departments (faculty) in the following areas is felt to be:
    a. Contribution of new works in performance and exhibits: very effective
    b. Development of an increasingly sophisticated laity (audience): moderately. People come here interested in the arts.
    c. Exploration of contemporary trends (arts movements):   moderately in music
    d. Vital, stimulating exploration of the heritage of each of the arts to introduce the seminal forces of the past: very effective
    e. Seeking new relationships in the arts: not enough

4. Do you feel your program is having any appreciable effect on the content and procedures of education in the arts in the schools — kindergarten through twelfth grade — in your state?
        Yes.

5. Admission for undergraduates in the arts is made:
   By the college.

6. A student major may be dropped from the departments:
   Because of grades below a certain point.

7. Admission to graduate work is made:
   By the graduate college.

8. Impact on the surrounding community by student and faculty artists
   is felt to be:
   Medium to strong.

9. Are you satisfied with your contribution to the number of "successful"
   working artists?
   Faculty: No.   Student: No.

Arts Events

1. Are you provided with funds in the budget over and above any box
   office returns to produce arts events?
   Yes.
   The budgets for this purpose annually amount to:
   Data not available—not broken out in the budgets.

2. Are the departments directly involved in the cultural events presented
   by off-campus artists:
   a. By having ex officio members on the "cultural presentations"
   committee?
   No.
   b. By directly relating these events to curricular work?
   No for all departments.

3. Total number of arts events (all arts) from off-campus for which
   tickets are sold:
   Over 100.
   Total admissions to arts events from off-campus: data not available

   Total income from arts events from off-campus: data not available

   Total expenses for arts events from off-campus: data not available

A sharp upswing in the arts on the Bloomington campus of Indiana
University began with Herman B. Wells' inauguration as president
in the late thirties and continues today with the strong support of
Mr. Wells, now in the role of chancellor, as well as that of the rest
of the administration. Except for architecture and film, there are
strong programs in all the arts with, perhaps, the largest budgets
in the country, especially for music. The School of Music has over
1,100 undergraduate majors and nearly 600 graduate majors; 115
faculty members and 240 student teaching assistants; 9,000 class
enrollments (this figure has been increasing at a rate of 15 percent
a year for five years); and a new music center opened in the spring
of 1972 that cost $10.1 million. The annual budget for the academic
arts programs for 1970–71 was $4.7 million. Another $175,000
was spent for the presentation of arts events from off-campus,
$150,000 of which was returned at the box office. These events
played to 55,000 admissions. In fact, the Bloomington campus is
the arts center for southern Indiana. An optimal enrollment of
majors has been determined in the very well developed music program, but the other departments are still working with this problem. A major, mature university, Indiana University provides an
extremely important illustration of how significantly the arts can
be developed on a large campus and serve the surrounding community in a rural region.

INDIANA UNIVERSITY

Administration

1. Year institution of higher education founded: 1820.

2. Departments in the arts formed:

Music	1910
Writing (courses)	1915
Visual arts	1939
Theater	1945

3. School of Music established in 1921.

4. Present administrative structure is due to: historical chance and powerful personality.

Student Personnel

1. Numbers of majors enrolled in the arts were:

Undergraduates	1971	1970	1969
Dance	57	53	22
Music	1,114	958	894
Theater	218	200	186
Visual arts	352	303	272
Writing*	26	44	30
TOTAL	1,767	1,558	1,404
Graduates	1971	1970	1969
Dance	7	5	7
Music	587	546	464
Theater	71	70	72
Visual arts	157	162	136
Writing*	14	13	23
TOTAL	836	796	702

* Figures for writing are not actually majors in a department of creative writing, but are English majors who take courses in creative writing.

2. Total numbers of class enrollments of all students (nonmajors and majors) in all classes in the fall term were:

Undergraduates	1971	1970	1969	1968	1967	1966
Dance	637	643	485	438	452	421
Music	6,944	6,153	5,932	6,201	5,963	5,532
Theater	921	946	890	815	740	665
Visual arts	2,929	1,936	1,950	2,488	2,302	
Writing	120	112	126	112	109	86
TOTAL	11,551	9,790	9,383	10,054	9,566	6,704
Graduates	1971	1970	1969	1968	1967	1966
Dance	*	59	58	56	54	82
Music	2,344	2,087	1,693	1,929	1,879	1,773
Theater	128	89	100	100	100	112
Visual arts	329	384	391	396	408	
Writing	14	13	23	15	19	17
TOTAL	2,815	2,632	2,265	2,496	2,460	1,984

* Summer session.

Faculty Personnel

	Number of full-time faculty FTE	Number of part-time faculty (bodies)	Sum of all FTEs	Number of student teaching assistants
Music (including dance)	113	4	115.00	240
Theater	34	1	34.25	33
Visual arts	36	1	36.50	43
Writing	13	7	14.88	8
TOTAL	196	13	200.63	324

Budget, 1970–71

	Amount of budget	Percentage for salaries	Percentage for operating expenses
Music (including dance)	$3,070,261	80	20
Theater	698,768	80	20
Visual arts	632,361	78	22
Writing	300,887	68	32
TOTAL	$4,702,277	79	21

Space and Equipment

1. The capital investment in buildings for the arts is:
    This breakdown of information is not available.

2. The number of square feet for specialized studio and laboratory use (other than general classroom space) is:

Dance	6,007
Music	69,635
Theater	8,843
Visual arts	58,788
TOTAL	143,273

3. *a.* Renovated square feet needed:
        17,098
    b. Additional square feet needed:
        42,033

4. Capital investment for special equipment is:

Music (including dance)	$1,263,939
Visual arts	1,205,671
TOTAL	$2,469,610

5. Projected costs of equipment needed for optimum operation are:
   Not answered.

Scholarships

The following undergraduate scholarships and graduate fellowships, teaching and otherwise, are awarded annually:

	Number of undergraduate scholarships	*Total amount in dollars*	*Number of graduate fellowships*	*Total amount in dollars*
Music	257	$ 91,137	36	$ 34,451
Theater			47	106,100
Visual arts			20	33,175
Writing	40	25,600	19	42,850
TOTAL	297	$116,737	122	$216,576

Qualitative Considerations

1. a. Is creative work considered equivalent to research in other disciplines as a criterion for promotion?
      Yes.
   b. Is an advanced academic degree required for appointment to the regular faculty?
      No.

2. Is there a growing question of the efficacy of tenure for faculty in the arts?
      No.

3. Effectiveness of the departments (faculty) in the following areas is felt to be:
   a. Contribution of new works in performance and exhibits: very effective
   b. Development of an increasingly sophisticated laity (audience): very effective
   c. Exploration of contemporary trends (arts movements): very effective

    d. Vital, stimulating exploration of the heritage of each of the arts to introduce the seminal forces of the past: very effective

    e. Seeking new relationships in the arts: very effective

4. Do you feel your program is having any appreciable effect on the content and procedures of education in the arts in the schools—kindergarten through twelfth grade—in your state?

    Yes.

5. Admission for undergraduates in the arts is made:

    With auditions and/or portfolio by the departments after admission to the university,

6. A student major may be dropped from the departments:

    Because of lack of talent and/or performance or because of grades below a certain point.

7. Admission to graduate work is made:

    With auditions and/or portfolio.

8. Impact on the surrounding community by student and faculty artists is felt to be:

    Strong.

9. Are you satisfied with your contribution to the number of "successful" working artists?

    Faculty: Yes.   Student: Yes.

Arts Events

1. Are you provided with funds in the budget over and above any box office returns to produce arts events?

    Not answered.

2. Are the departments directly involved in the cultural events presented by off-campus artists:

    a. By having ex officio members on the "cultural presentations" committee?

        Yes.

    b. By directly relating these events to curricular work?

        Yes for all departments.

3. Total number of arts events (all arts) from off-campus for which tickets are sold:

    29,

Total admissions to arts events from off-campus: 54,514

Total income from arts events from off-campus: $149,979

Total expenses for arts events from off-campus: $174,668

4. Estimates of the percentage breakdown of attendance between *(a)* students and faculty and *(b)* the community at major on-campus events of the following types are.

	Student/Faculty (percent)	Community (percent)
Music and dance	80	20
Theater	71	29

JACKSON STATE COLLEGE The state of Mississippi has both maintained and limited the development of Jackson State College, and, until recently, the arts have had little opportunity to grow. The following responses to the questionnaire illustrate this fact. There is no studio space, for example, and classrooms are used for studio purposes. Only music, theater, and the visual arts are offered, with some creative writing in the English department. In comparison with the arts at Fisk University, another predominately black campus in the South, the arts at Jackson State are just beginning to develop. But the dean here gets high marks for his support, and a building program is slated for 1972–73. Jackson State has provided the large majority of black teachers in the state over the years, and it is encouraging to note that the arts are coming into their own on campus. So far dance and film have not been part of the scene, and it is to be hoped that these two significant arts in today's world will be available to students before long.

JACKSON STATE COLLEGE

Administration

1. Year institution of higher education founded: 1877.

2. Departments in the arts formed:

Music	1887
Visual arts	1949
Theater	1971

3. No separate administrative unit for the arts.

4. Present administrative structure is due to: tradition.

Student Personnel

1. Numbers of majors enrolled in the arts were:

Undergraduates	*1971*	*1970*	*1969*
Music	120	114	105
Visual arts	135	116	114
TOTAL	255	230	219

No graduate students

NOTE: Forty-eight minors in theater reported for 1971.

2. Total numbers of class enrollments of all students (nonmajors and majors) in all classes in the fall term were:

Undergraduates	*1971*
Music	1,215
Theater	40
Visual arts	768
TOTAL	2,023

No graduate students

NOTE: Figures for years 1966–1970 not reported.

Faculty Personnel

	Number of full-time faculty FTE	*Number of part-time faculty (bodies)*	*Sum of all FTEs*
Music	19		19
Theater	1	2	2
Visual arts	8	—	8
TOTAL	28	2	29

NOTE: Number of student teaching assistants not reported.

Budget, 1970–71

	Amount of budget	*Percentage for salaries*	*Percentage for operating expenses*
Film	$ 1,499	0.0	100.0
Music	220,627	74.7	25.3
Visual arts	65,127	92.7	7.3
TOTAL	$287,253	83.7	16.3

Space and Equipment

1. The capital investment in buildings for the sum of the departments in the arts is:

    None. Building program planned for 1972–73 academic year.

2. The number of square feet for specialized studio and laboratory use (other than general classroom space) is:

    At present classrooms are used for studio purposes.

3. Capital investment for special equipment is:

Music	$24,616
Visual arts	1,067
TOTAL	$25,683

Scholarships

The following undergraduate scholarships are awarded annually:

	Number	*Total amount in dollars*
Music	40	$17,609
Visual arts	4	2,050
TOTAL	44	$19,659

Qualitative Considerations

1. *a.* Is creative work considered equivalent to research in other disciplines as a criterion for promotion?
   Yes.
   b. Is an advanced academic degree required for appointment to the regular faculty?
   Yes. Master of Arts.

2. Is there a growing question of the efficacy of tenure for faculty in the arts in your college?
   No.

3. Effectiveness of departments (faculty) in the following areas is felt to be:
   a. Contribution of new works in performance and exhibits: moderately
   b. Development of an increasingly sophisticated laity (audience): moderately
   c. Exploration of contemporary trends (arts movements): moderately
   d. Vital, stimulating exploration of the heritage of each of the arts to introduce the seminal forces of the past: moderately
   e. Seeking new relationships in the arts: moderately

4. Do you feel your college is having any appreciable effect on the content and procedures of education in the arts in the schools—kindergarten through twelfth grade—in your state?
   Yes

5. Admission for undergraduates in the arts is made:
    By the college admissions in consultation with the departments, and with auditions and/or portfolio.

6. A student major may be dropped from the college or department:
    Because of grades below a certain point.

7. Impact on the surrounding community by student and faculty artists is felt to be:
    Medium.

8. Are you satisfied with your contribution to the number of "successful" working artists?
    Faculty: No.   Student: Not answered.

Arts Events

1. Are you provided with funds in the budget over and above any box office returns to produce arts events?
    Yes.
    The budgets for this purpose annually amount to:
    Response unclear.

2. Are the arts directly involved in the cultural events presented by off-campus artists:
    a. By having ex officio members on the "cultural presentations" committee?
    Not answered.

    b. By directly relating these events to curricular work?

Dance	Yes
Film	Yes
Music	Yes
Theater	Yes
Writing	Yes
Visual arts	Yes

3. Total number of arts events (all arts) from off-campus for which tickets are sold:
    Not reported.

4. Estimates of the percentage breakdown of attendance between *(a)* students and faculty and *(b)* the community at major on-campus events of the following type are:
    Not reported.

**NEW YORK
UNIVERSITY** The arts at NYU have a crazy quilt pattern—they are spread throughout the university and appear in all different types of administrative arrangements. The School of the Arts offers dance, film, and theater. Washington Square College has a department of fine arts, which is an art history department, and a department of music, known for musicology. The Institute of Fine Arts is a well-respected graduate research-oriented facility concerned with art history, archaeology, and conservation. The School of Education administers art education and music education, which include studio courses. Noncredit courses and special events are handled by the School of Continuing Education. The Town Hall, a metropolitan center for concerts, political and other lectures, films, dance, and some theater, is also a unit of the School of Continuing Education. In 1971, a joint program to train administrators of the performing arts was set up by the Town Hall and the department of music education. The New York University Art Collection is a separate administrative entity which serves the entire university. And all this does not mention the arts at NYU's University Heights campus in the Bronx.

Since about 1969, NYU as a whole has been undergoing a severe crisis, marked especially by a drastic drop-off in undergraduate enrollment. The NYU Task Force on the Financial Emergency, composed of five academic deans and a vice-chancellor for administration, has now recommended that undergraduate faculty and services be reduced by 50 percent because of this development. In this context, one would expect a general cutback of the arts across the board, but this is not the case. Some units continue to be strong and others wilt. The School of the Arts has shown a consistent pattern of growth. Its undergraduate class enrollments rose from 2,440 in the fall of 1969 to 3,180 in 1971. The Institute of Fine Arts is also growing. But courses in both of the departments in Washington Square College and in the School of Continuing Education have decreasing enrollments—of at least several hundred in each case. Town Hall is growing. Though it provides facilities to artists at the lowest rental rate of any major concert hall in the New York area and charges modest admission prices, it is currently decreasing its deficit, which is covered by the university. It has been granted new funds from private and governmental sources and is now organizing a board of private citizens to help with support. The School of Education did not report on its program.

The NYU administration should perhaps consider the current

functions of its highly respected units in the arts as a basis for a new administrative unit rather than continue with a traditional apparatus, constructed to serve the arts in former times.

NEW YORK UNIVERSITY

Administration

1. Year institution of higher education founded: 1831.

2. Departments in the arts formed:

*Visual arts**	1832
Music, Washington Square College	1923
School of Continuing Education, with courses in the arts	1933
Institute of Fine Arts	1938
NYU Art Collection	1958
Town Hall, absorbed into NYU	1958
Dance	1966
Film	1967
Theater	1967

* The Chair of Sculpture and Painting, established in 1832 and held by Samuel F. B. Morse, was the first fine arts chair in the United States.

3. The School of the Arts was established in 1965. It now includes the departments of dance, film, and theater. The dean of the school reports to the chancellor.

4. Present administrative structure is due to: a combination of historical chance, powerful personality, and careful design.

Student Personnel

1. Numbers of majors enrolled in the arts were:

Undergraduates	1971	1970	1969
School of the Arts			
Dance	45	35	35
Film	427	412	350
Theater	140	140	135
TOTAL	612	587	520
Washington Square College			
Fine arts	100*	†	120*
Music	24	18	16
TOTAL	124*		136*

Graduates	1971	1970	1969
School of the Arts			
Dance	15	10	10
Film	60	55	50
Theater	35	30	25
TOTAL	110	95	85
Washington Square College			
Music	81	77	85
Institute of Fine Arts	256	230	209

*Figures approximate.
† Not available.
NOTE: The School of Education did not report.

2. Total numbers of class enrollments of all students (nonmajors and majors) in the fall term were:

Undergraduates	1971	1970	1969	1968	1967	1966
School of the Arts						
Dance	180	140	140	120	120	120
Film	1,800	1,500	1,200	1,000	800	600
Theater	1,200	1,200	1,100	1,100	1,150	1,050
TOTAL	3,180	2,840	2,440	2,220	2,070	1,770
Washington Square College						
Fine arts	700*	†	900*			
Music	453	466	534	843	684	576
TOTAL	1,153*		1,434*			

Graduates	1971	1970	1969	1968	1967	1966
School of the Arts						
Dance	60	40	40	40	40	40
Film	700	650	500	400	160	0
Theater	250	220	200	200	180	100
TOTAL	1,010	910	740	640	380	140
Washington Square College						
Music	148	179	183	158	181	163

* Figures approximate.
† Not available.
NOTE: The School of Education did not report.

Noncredit courses, School of Continuing Education, division of liberal studies

	1971	1970	1969	1968	1967	1966
Architecture	26	27	28	14	22	23
Dance	95	50	98	79	55	19
Film	531	545	309	342	159	138
Music	332	288	371	423	367	363
Theater	51	68	92	28	30	33
Visual arts	529	676	740	742	662	509
Writing	340	574	787	491	650	574
TOTAL	1,904	2,228	2,425	2,119	1,945	1,659

Faculty Personnel

	Number of full-time faculty FTE	Number of part-time faculty (bodies)	Number of student teaching assistants
School of the Arts			
Dance	5	7	2
Film	20	21	10
Theater	23	15	6
TOTAL	48	43	18
Washington Square College			
Fine arts	4	10	3
Music	12	2	5
TOTAL	16	12	8
Institute of Fine Arts	14	19	

Budget, 1970–71

	Amount of budget	Percentage for salaries	Percentage for operating expenses
School of the Arts			
Dance	$ 64,606	80	20
Film	518,840	55	45
Theater	602,779	70	30
Sum of departments	$1,186,225		
Administrative & general expenses	348,181		
TOTAL	$1,534,406		
Washington Square College			
Fine arts	$ 240,000		
Music	*		
Institute of Fine Arts	$ 674,708†		
School of Continuing Education			
Division of liberal studies	$ 300,000	75	25
Special events	63,000		
Town Hall	327,179		
TOTAL	$ 690,179		
NYU Art Collection	$ 65,000		

* Figure withheld.
† Plus outside funding of $658,013.

Space and Equipment

1. The capital investment for buildings in the arts is:

School of the Arts	
Dance	$ 500,000
Film	1,500,000
Theater	1,500,000
TOTAL	$3,500,000
Institute of Fine Arts	$3,850,000
School of Continuing Education	
Division of liberal studies	$ 350,000*
Town Hall	850,000
TOTAL	$, ,

* All classes, except two art studios, are held in general university buildings or in off-campus rented facilities.

2. The number of square feet for specialized studio and laboratory use (other than general classroom space) is:

School of the Arts	
Dance	8,000
Film	12,000
Theater	20,000
TOTAL	40,000
Institute of Fine Arts	14,000
School of Continuing Education	
Division of liberal studies	2,500 (plus rented space)

3. *a.* Renovated square feet needed:
      3,500 (School of the Arts)
   b. Additional square feet needed:

School of the Arts	40,000
Institute of Fine Arts	7,000 (minimum)
School of Continuing Education	
Division of liberal studies	20,000
*Special events**	3,000
NYU Art Collection	10,000

*Special events indicates need for audiovisual equipment not now available. Since present facilities for events cannot store this equipment, purchase is not anticipated.

4. Capital investment for special equipment is:

School of the Arts	
Dance	$ 20,000
Film	450,000
Theater	150,000
TOTAL	$ 620,000
Institute of Fine Arts	$ 740,000
School of Continuing Education	
Division of liberal studies	$ 10,000 (film)
Town Hall	100,000
TOTAL	$110,000

5. Projected costs of equipment needed for optimum operation are:

School of the Arts

Dance	$ 10,000
Film	200,000
Theater	50,000
TOTAL	$ 260,000
Institute of Fine Arts	$ 42,500 (per year)
School of Continuing Education	
Division of liberal studies	$ 150,000 (film)

Scholarships

The following undergraduate scholarships and graduate fellowships, teaching and otherwise, are awarded annually:

	Number of undergraduate scholarships	*Total amount in dollars*	*Number of graduate fellowships*	*Total amount in dollars*
School of the Arts				
Dance	9	$18,000	3	$ 6,000
Film	10	20,000	8	16,000
Theater	20	40,000	10	20,000
TOTAL	39	$78,000	21	$ 42,000
Washington Square College				
Fine arts			3	
Music			7.5	$ 14,220
Institute of Fine Arts			95	$148,500
NYU Art Collection			1–2	

Qualitative Considerations

1. *a.* Is creative work considered equivalent to research in other disciplines as a criterion for promotion?
   Yes.
   b. Is an advanced academic degree required for appointment to the regular faculty?
   No.

2. Is there a growing question of the efficacy of tenure for faculty in the arts in your university?

    No.

3. Effectiveness of the departments (faculty) in the following areas is felt to be:
    a. Contribution of new works in performance and exhibits: moderately
    b. Development of an increasingly sophisticated laity (audience): no way of judging
    c. Exploration of contemporary trends (arts movements): moderately
    d. Vital, stimulating exploration of the heritage of each of the arts to introduce the seminal forces of the past: very effective
    e. Seeking new relationships in the arts: moderately

4. Do you feel your program is having any appreciable effect on the content and procedures of education in the arts in the schools— kindergarten through twelfth grade—in your state?

    School of the arts: No. (The School of Education did not report.)

5. Admission for undergraduates in the arts is made:

    School of the Arts: By the school, with auditions and/or portfolio.

6. A student major may be dropped from the college or department:

    Because of lack of talent and/or performance or because of grades below a certain level.

7. Admission to graduate work is made:

    School of the Arts: By the school, with auditions and/or portfolio.

8. Impact on the surrounding community by student and faculty artists is felt to be:

    School of the Arts: Weak. Our school is located in the heart of professional dance, film, and theater activity.

9. Are you satisifed with your contribution to the number of "successful" working artists?

    Faculty: Yes.   Student: Yes.

Arts Events

1. Are you provided with funds in the budget over and above any box office returns to produce arts events?
   Yes.

   The budgets for this purpose annually amount to:

School of the Arts

Dance	$ 4,000
Film	8,000
Theater	12,000
TOTAL	$24,000

School of Continuing Education

Special Events	$39,800

2. Is the school and/or the departments directly involved in the cultural events presented by off-campus artists:
   a. By having ex officio members on the "cultural presentations" committee?
      No.
   b. By directly relating these events to curricular work?
      Yes, in dance, film, and theater.

3. Total number of arts events (all arts) from off-campus for which tickets are sold:
      62 (1971–72 academic year).

   Total admissions to arts events from off-campus: Approximately 15,000

   Total income from arts events from off-campus: Estimated $23,500

   Total expenses for arts events from off-campus: Estimated $63,300

4. Estimates of the percentage breakdown of attendance between *(a)* students and faculty and *(b)* the community at major on-campus events of the following type are:

	Student/Faculty (percent)	Community (percent)
Dance	50	50
Film	80	20
Music	50	50
Theater	60	40
Visual arts	25	75
Writing	25	75

PASADENA
CITY COLLEGE
If the high school can be considered the mother who nurtured the community college, the university was the old-fashioned father who insisted for so many years that those students who were not "college material" be kept out of his hair. But the community college has come of age and its major identity crisis is over, at least conceptually. Its mission is understood to be universal education and self-discovery for all adults through college transfer programs, occupational training programs, guidance, continuing education, and community service. It now remains to be seen how well the community college can carry out this mission.

The arts have always been involved in the 70 years of growth in the community college, but as with society-at-large, they have been considered more peripheral than integral. For example, in a recently published book on the community college, Charles Monroe (1972, p. 391) emphasizes the arts as extremely important, particularly as a co-curricular activity. When speaking of future developments, however, he mentions that "the community-college movement may be affected by competing *economic* and *social* forces" but does not mention cultural (aesthetic) forces. (Italics are mine.)

With the impressive statistics of past, present, and projected future growth of the community college—over 1,000 institutions and 2 million students in 1970 and forecasts that by 1975 over half of the freshmen in the country will be in community colleges and that by 1980 this number will rise to three-quarters—a conscious determination of a policy for education in all the arts is vital and formal study of inherent problems past due.

Pasadena City College, an active agent in the development of the community college since its establishment in 1924, was chosen as an example of this type of institution for inclusion in this study along with other highly diverse schools. At the present time, there is even less information available about the arts in the community college than there is about the arts in four-year colleges and universities, and one case is not presumed to do justice to all but does call attention to the field. The work at Pasadena in the arts provides a concrete example of the extent of the arts in one school. Other community colleges report that often their courses in the arts are "the first to fill up." One administrator said, "The students are restoring the arts to the center of the curriculum." Some teachers in the arts are convinced that the arts constitute an important force which is currently reordering values in our society and find this a strong stimulant which motivates their teaching. And more adults are coming to the campus for arts events as well as classes. Pasadena reflects this trend. It should be noted that the allocation of teaching personnel, space, and financial resources at Pasadena is more extensive than at some "great universities."

PASADENA CITY COLLEGE

Administration

1. Year institution of higher education founded: 1924.

2. Departments in the arts formed:

Music	1927
Visual arts	1927
Dance	1948
Architecture	1957
Theater	1958

3. No separate administrative units for the arts.

4. Present administrative structure due to: tradition.

Student Personnel

1. Numbers of majors enrolled in the arts were:

Undergraduates	*1971*	*1970*	*1969*
Architecture	121	142	130
Music	376	202	142
Theater*	68	90	66
Visual arts	702	647	607
Writing†	55	42	45
Apparel arts‡	66	87	111
Photography‡	83	91	88
Radio and TV	212	145	154
Sign art (Graphics)	26	26	23
TOTAL	1,709	1,472	1,366

No graduate students

* Theater is in the communications department.
† Writing is in the English department.
‡ Photography and apparel arts are in the art department.

2. Total numbers of class enrollments of all students (nonmajors and majors) in all classes in the fall term were:

Undergraduates	1971	1970	1969	1968	1967	1966
Architecture	286	364	310	408	318	247
Music	1,964	1,719	1,285	1,582	1,356	1,037
Theater	257	272	273	211	156	88
Visual arts	3,015	2,118	2,043	1,727	1,813	1,184
Writing	119	124	125	98	100	64
Apparel arts	302	293	249	191	222	134
Dance*	482	498	470	372	387	149
Photography	279	266	202	149	154	101
Radio and TV	535	469	377	323	266	192
Sign art	71	73	67	65	80	48
TOTAL	7,310	6,196	5,401	5,126	4,852	3,244

No graduate students

*Dance is in the physical education department.

Faculty Personnel

	Number of full-time faculty FTE	Number of part-time faculty (bodies)	Sum of all FTE's	Number of student teaching assistants
Architecture	3	2	4.00	
Music	10	1	10.50	1
Theater	1	3	2.40	
Visual arts*			15.95	1
Writing	1	2	2.20	
Dance		3	1.85	
Photography	2		2.00	1
Radio and TV	4		4.00	3.5
TOTAL			42.90	6.5

*Only FTE total reported.

Budget, 1970–71

	Amount of budget	Percentage for salaries	Percentage for operating expenses
Architecture	$ 76,538	85	15
Music	187,692	76	24
Theater	43,031	85	15
Visual arts	291,579	72	28
Writing	35,362	90	10
Dance	29,397	89	11
Photography	36,038	75	25
Radio and TV	38,459	70	30
TOTAL	$738,096	85	15

Space and Equipment

1. The capital investment in buildings for departments in the arts is:

Architecture	$ 50,000
Music	400,000
Theater	300,000
Visual arts	1,300,000
Dance	50,000
Photography	100,000
TOTAL	$2,200,000

2. The number of square feet for specialized studio and laboratory use (other than general classroom space) is:

Architecture	1,954
Music	11,187
Theater	17,423
Visual arts	22,629
Dance	4,186
Photography	3,498
Other (unspecified)	9,123
TOTAL	70,000

3. *a.* Renovated square feet needed:
32,903

　　b.　Additional square feet needed:
　　　　30,000

4.　Capital investment for special equipment is:

Architecture	$　25,000
Music	75,000
Theater	30,000
Writing	5,000
Visual arts	50,000
Dance	15,000
Photography	60,000
Radio and TV	500,000
TOTAL	$760,000

5.　Projected costs of equipment needed for optimum operation are:

Architecture	$　　500
Music	3,300
Theater	1,900
Writing	3,500
Visual arts	6,000
Dance	100
Photography	1,942
Radio and TV	175,000
TOTAL	$192,242

Scholarships

Not applicable. The Pasadena Arts Council each year gives three $150 awards for art, drama, and music.

Qualitative Considerations

1.　*a.*　Is creative work considered equivalent to research in other disciplines as a criterion for promotion?
　　　　Not applicable. Teaching ability is the sole criterion throughout the college.
　　b.　Is an advanced academic degree required for appointment to the regular faculty?
　　　　Yes

2. Is there a growing question of the efficacy of tenure for faculty in the arts?

    No.

3. Effectiveness of the departments (faculty) in the following areas is felt to be:

    a. Contribution of new works in performance and exhibits: moderately

    b. Development of an increasingly sophisticated laity (audience): not enough

    c. Exploration of contemporary trends (arts movements): very effective

    d. Vital, stimulating exploration of the heritage of each of the arts to introduce the seminal forces of the past: very effective

    e. Seeking new relationships in the arts: moderately

4. Do you feel your program is having any appreciable effect on the content and procedures of education in the arts in the schools—kindergarten through twelfth grade—in your state?

    Yes. But needs improvement through increased contact with the faculty of these schools.

5. Admission for undergraduates in the arts is made:

    By the college admissions office without recourse to the departments.

6. A student major may be dropped from the departments:

    Because of grades below a certain point.

7. Impact on the surrounding community by student and faculty artists is felt to be:

    Medium.

8. Are you satisfied with your contribution to the number of "successful" working artists?

    Faculty: Yes.   Student: Yes.

Arts Events

1. Are you provided with funds in the budget over and above any box office returns to produce arts events?

    Yes, only as part of the instructional program for students. Costs of such events are borne by the college as part of the operational budget.

2. Are the departments directly involved in the cultural events presented by off-campus artists:
   a. By having ex officio members on the "cultural presentations" committee?
      Yes.
   b. By directly relating these events to curricular work?
      Yes in all areas except theater.

3. Total number of arts events (all arts) from off-campus for which tickets are sold:
      None.

4. Estimates of the percentage breakdown of attendance between *(a)* students and faculty and *(b)* the community at major on-campus events of the following type are:

	Student/Faculty (percent)	Community (percent)
Architecture	40	60
Dance	50	50
Photography	40	60
Music	30	70
Theater	20	80
Writing	20	80

84345

PENNSYL-
VANIA STATE
UNIVERSITY

The College of Arts and Architecture at Penn State is one of the most comprehensive administrative units in the arts in a university offering both undergraduate and graduate work. (Dance and film are not separate units within the college, but are included in theater arts.) The dean of the college also administers the Artists Series and the University Gallery and art exhibitions, and he is directly responsible to the president. Since it is located in a relatively remote area, the college does not have the resources in the arts of a major city and, therefore, must provide such offerings itself. The college plans to try to meet this need, and the dean projects that the total of class enrollments and admissions at arts events will be 500,000 at full operation.

Students in art education and music education are not enrolled in the College of Arts and Architecture, but in the College of Education, whose department of art education has a distinguished history in its field. This separation of art and art education, due to tradition, illustrates a current problem which has not been treated to careful study: What are the conditions which serve teacher training in the arts most effectively, a major in a college of the arts or a major in a college of education?

PENNSYLVANIA STATE UNIVERSITY

Administration

1. Year institution of higher education founded: 1855.

2. Departments in the arts formed:

Music	1915
Dramatics	1919
Architecture	1922
Theater	1954
Visual arts	1956
Landscape architecture	1963
Art history	1964

3. College of Arts and Architecture established in 1963. The dean reports to the president and the provost.

4.   Present administrative structure is due to: careful design.

Student Personnel

1.   Numbers of majors enrolled in the arts were:

Undergraduates	1971	1970	1969
Architecture	372	428	443
Music	65	73	61
Theater*	196	178	148
Visual arts	289	242	211
Art history	29	26	49
Landscape architecture	137	138	149
TOTAL	1,088	1,085	1,061

Graduates	1971	1970	1969
Architecture	12	3	6
Music	26	12	24
Theater*	56	53	52
Visual arts	21	22	26
Art history	75	45	33
Regional planning		32	28
TOTAL	190	167	169

*Includes dance, film, and writing.

2.   Total numbers of class enrollments of all students (nonmajors and majors) in the fall term were:

Undergraduates	1971	1970	1969	1968	1967	1966
Architecture	826	879	1,136	1,091	510	362
Music	1,620	1,390	1,346	1,294	1,289	1,279
Theater	2,330	1,962	1,567	2,151	1,345	738
Visual arts	1,173	955	950	956	970	744
Art history	866	768	1,029	825	910	856
General education in the arts	356	362	358	337	214	294
Landscape architecture	341	424	460	541	511	486
TOTAL	7,512	6,740	6,846	7,195	5,749	4,759

Graduates	1971	1970	1969	1968	1967	1966
Architecture	14	66	8	9	1	1
Music	84	33	61	37	16	16
Theater	113	131	83	71	56	45
Visual arts	36	27	33	29	33	25
Art history	97	63	54	41	42	35
Regional planning		96	82	45	49	10
TOTAL	344	416	321	232	197	132

Faculty Personnel

	Number of full-time faculty FTE	Number of part-time faculty (bodies)	Number of student teaching assistants
Architecture	17		4
Music	22	1	17
Theater	19	5	4
Visual arts	17	9	7
Art history	9		2
General education in the arts	2		2
Landscape architecture	10		
TOTAL	96	15	36

Budget, 1970–71

	Amount of budget	Percentage for salaries	Percentage for operating expenses
Architecture	$ 285,000	96	4
Music	380,000	97	3
Theater	487,000	78	22
Visual arts	337,000	97	3
Art history	199,000	96	4
General education in the arts	49,000	97	3
Landscape architecture	159,000	94	6
Regional planning	41,000	95	5
Subtotal	$1,937,000		
Administration	142,000	91	9
Artists series	118,000	33	67

	Amount of budget	Percentage for salaries	Percentage for operating expenses
Continuing education	36,000	73	27
Research	19,000	32	68
Reserve	119,000	50	50
University gallery and exhibitions	44,000	70	30
TOTAL	$2,415,000	86	14

Space and Equipment

1. The capital investment for total College of Arts and Architecture buildings is:

Architecture	$ 443,527
Music	933,611
Theater	1,422,030
Visual arts	3,449,951
Art history	129,473
General education in the arts	16,672
Landscape architecture	219,646
Subtotal	$6,614,910
Artists series	36,101
Gallery space	935,335
Offices	140,414
TOTAL	$7,726,760

2. The number of square feet for specialized studio and laboratory use (other than general classroom space) is:

Architecture	19,800
Music	21,300
Theater	34,000
Visual arts	28,500
Art history	400
Landscape architecture	7,000
TOTAL	111,000

3. *a.* Renovated square feet needed:
       46,200
    b. Additional square feet needed:
       169,500

4. Capital investment for special equipment is:

Architecture (including landscape architecture)	$ 90,000
Music	242,000
Theater	450,000
Visual arts	250,000
Art history	60,000
Subtotal	$1,092,000
Artists series	20,000
Exhibitions	200,000
Offices	38,000
TOTAL	$1,350,000

5. Projected costs of equipment needed for optimum operation are:

Architecture	$ 25,000
Music	30,000
Theater	100,000
Visual arts	60,000
Art history	20,000
Landscape architecture	30,000
TOTAL	$265,000

Scholarships

The following undergraduate scholarships and graduate fellowships, teaching and otherwise, are awarded annually:

	Number of undergraduate scholarships	Total amount in dollars	Number of graduate fellowships	Total amount in dollars
Architecture	1	$ 250	4	$ 8,280
Music	4	330	17	17,200
Theater	2	700	21	43,470
Visual arts	2	550	15	16,200
Art history	1	250	16	18,600
General education in the arts			10	20,700
Landscape architecture	1	150		
TOTAL	11	$2,230	83	$124,450

Qualitative Considerations

1. *a.* Is creative work considered equivalent to research in other disciplines as a criterion for promotion?
   Yes.
   b. Is an advanced academic degree required for appointment to the regular faculty?
   No.

2. Is there a growing question of the efficacy of tenure for faculty in the arts?
   Yes. Various departments have limited success in establishing measurable criteria for tenure.

3. Effectiveness of the departments (faculty) in the following areas is felt to be:
   a. Contribution of new works in performance and exhibits: moderately
   b. Development of an increasingly sophisticated laity (audience):   very effective
   c. Exploration of contemporary trends (arts movements):   moderately
   d. Vital, stimulating exploration of the heritage of each of the arts to introduce the seminal forces of the past: not enough
   e. Seeking new relationships in the arts: moderately

4. Do you feel your program is having any appreciable effect on the content and procedures of education in the arts in the schools—kindergarten through twelfth grade—in your state?

No. Art education and music education are not in the College of Arts and Architecture, but in the College of Education.

5. Admission for undergraduates in the arts is made:
By the university admissions in consultation with the college, by the college after admission to the university, and with auditions and/or portfolio.

6. A student major may be dropped from the college or department:
Because of lack of talent and/or performance or because of grades below a certain point.

7. Admission to graduate work is made:
By the Graduate School with the recommendation of the college. The department responsible has the final say in admission.

8. Impact on the surrounding community by student and faculty artists is felt to be:
Strong.

9. Are you satisfied with your contribution to the number of "successful" working artists?
Faculty: No.   Student: No.

Arts Events

1. Are you provided with funds in the budget over and above any box office returns to produce arts events?
Yes.

The budgets for this purpose annually amount to:

Theater	$ 65,000
Visual arts (university gallery and exhibitions)	44,000
Artists series	75,000
TOTAL	$184,000

2. Is the college and/or the departments directly involved in the cultural events presented by off-campus artists:
   a. By having ex officio members on the "cultural presentations" committee?
   Yes. The dean of the College of Arts and Architecture is chairman.
   b. By directly relating these events to curricular work?
   Yes in all areas except film.

3. Total number of arts events (all arts) from off-campus for which tickets are sold:
    19.

    Total admissions to arts events from off-campus: 60,000

    Total income from arts events from off-campus: $83,500

    Total expenses for arts events from off-campus: $160,500

4. Estimates of the percentage breakdown of attendance between *(a)* students and faculty and *(b)* the community at major on-campus events of the following type are:

	Student/Faculty (percent)	Community (percent)
Architecture	85	15
Dance	75	25
Film	60	40
Music	50	50
Theater	60	40
Visual arts	80	20
Artists series	70	30
Exhibitions	75	25
Landscape architecture	95	5

UNIVERSITY OF
CALIFORNIA
AT LOS
ANGELES The College of Fine Arts at UCLA was formed in 1960 from the College of Applied Arts which, in addition to art and music, included ROTC, nursing, and physical education. When the School of Architecture was added to the university six years later, it was not included in the college. The College of Fine Arts now has four departments: music (begun in 1919), art (1920), theater arts, including film and television (1947), and dance (1962).

Since World War II, the arts have had strong campuswide support and notable backing from the university's chief administrators: Chancellors Clarence A. Dykstra, Vern O. Knudsen, and Franklin Murphy, as well as Presidents Robert Gordon Sproul and Clark Kerr. The college's budget for 1972 is over $4 million, and its capital investment in building is reportedly over $8 million, providing more than 230,000 square feet of space.

The four arts departments, the Grunewald Gallery, the art gallery, the Museum of Culture, and the Institute of Ethnomusicology all report to the dean of the College of Fine Arts.

Related to the college but entirely independent is the Committee of Fine Arts Productions, which provides campuswide arts events for the campus and the surrounding community. The remarkable growth of campuswide arts events has been documented by both the Committee of Fine Arts Productions and the Campus Activities Service Office[3] (formerly the department of central stage management), which provides the complete range of services needed for performance in the various theaters and auditoriums. This latter organization schedules all nonclass activities in all facilities on campus. Between 1959–60 and 1969–70, attendance for all events provided by the Committee of Fine Arts Productions grew from 160,000 to 330,000, with a peak year in 1965–66 of 447,000. The growth for each type of event for the same 10-year period breaks down as follows (figures are rounded to the nearest 1,000):

[3] The following data was provided to the author by Frances Inglis, executive officer of the Committee of Fine Arts Productions, and James Klain, director of the Campus Activities Service Office.

	1959–60	1969–70
Art	23,000	72,000
Concerts	26,000	137,000
Dance	3,000	5,000
Films	30,000	34,000
Junior programs (for children)	15,000	14,000
Music	18,000	25,000
Theater arts	14,000	20,000

During its existence, the professional UCLA Theater Group attracted an audience that grew from 16,000 in 1959–60 to 50,000 in 1966, with a peak year in 1965–66 of 83,000. (The UCLA Theater Group was transferred to the Los Angeles Music Center, where it became the resident producing organization under the direction of Gordon Davidson in 1968–69.)

The Campus Activities Service Office can provide an even longer record—from 1947–48 with 58,000 admissions to 1970–71 with 315,000 admissions, or an increase of 440 percent. The rise of the arts on the UCLA campus reflects the similar growth throughout the country of large metropolitan universities which serve as centers for the arts in their communities. Other colleges and universities of various sizes and locales (rural, semirural, suburban, exurban, and urban) have experienced similar growth and impact. And while officials at UCLA report serious restraints and crippling difficulties due to the budget cutbacks of the state legislature under Governor Ronald Reagan, the campus nevertheless continues to be an extremely strong force in the West Los Angeles area. Many feel, however, that UCLA, like other major universities with a strong arts component, has yet to reach the same effective level in providing new works, fresh talent, and innovative approaches in the arts as it has reached in the areas of physics, engineering, biology, and other disciplines. The impact on our culture of the work in and with the arts of colleges and universities across the country has not been assessed or fully understood; but many students, faculty, and officials feel that their work is a real force in the changing of values in our society, one component of what is being recognized as a "cultural revolution."

UNIVERSITY OF CALIFORNIA AT LOS ANGELES

Administration

1. Year institution of higher education founded: 1882

2. Departments in the arts formed:

Music	1919
Visual arts	1920
Theater	1947
Dance	1962

3. College of Fine Arts established in 1960. The dean reports to the vice-chancellor.

4. Present administrative structure is due to: careful design.

Student Personnel

1. Numbers of majors enrolled in the arts were:

Undergraduates	*1971*	*1970*	*1969‡*
Dance	83	117	125
Music	255	294	342
*Theater**	429	552	662
Visual arts†	616	626	921
TOTAL	1,383	1,589	2,050
Graduates	*1971*	*1970*	*1969‡*
Dance	75	60	52
Music	111	121	133
Theater	257	259	308
Visual arts	228	250	238
TOTAL	671	690	731

* Includes film.

† Includes art history.

‡ The year 1969 represents the peak of an "overenrollment" problem, which was cut back by various methods of control in 1970.

NOTE: Information on the School of Architecture is not provided.

2. Total numbers of class enrollments of all students (nonmajors and majors) in the fall term were:

Undergraduates	1971	1970	1969	1968	1967	1966
Dance	781	895	888	673	418	438
Music	2,883	2,835	3,323	3,272	3,212	2,425
Theater	2,000	2,313	2,373	1,936	1,808	1,413
Visual arts	2,400	2,919	3,182	2,997	2,783	2,700
Integrated arts	312	441	386	424	281	186
TOTAL	8,376	9,403	10,152	9,302	8,502	7,162
Graduates	1971	1970	1969	1968	1967	1966
Dance	89	93	46	48	44	21
Music	135	129	126	129	109	102
Theater	385	355	452	386	371	284
Visual arts	336	421	416	380	346	266
TOTAL	945	998	1,040	943	870	673

Faculty Personnel

	Number of full-time faculty FTE	Number of part-time faculty (bodies)	Sum of all FTE's	Number of student teaching assistants
Dance	3*	11	17.50	4.50
	6†			
Music	6*	34	70.65	15.35
	38†			
Theater	11*	24	64.75	15.75
	24†			
Visual arts	17*	19	77.62	20.00
	35†			
TOTAL	140	88	230.52	55.60

* Temporary.
† Permanent.

Budget, 1970–71

	Amount of budget
Dance	$ 254,119
Music	1,189,318
Theater	1,088,092
Visual arts	980,487
Sum of departments	530,695
*Other college expenses**	$3,512,016
TOTAL	$4,042,711

*Includes dean's office and partial funding of galleries, museums and Institute of Ethnomusicology.

NOTE: Percentages for salaries and for operating expenses not reported.

Space and Equipment

1. The capital investment for total college buildings is:
       Not answered.

2. The number of square feet of space in the college is:

Dance	10,564
Music	32,686
Theater	85,775
Visual arts	59,166
Sum of departments	188,191
Dean's office	2,400
Grunewald Gallery	2,100
Art museum	10,400
Museum of Culture	21,900
Institute of Ethnomusicology	4,700
TOTAL	229,691

3. Additional square feet needed:
       Not answered.

4. Capital investment for special equipment is:
       Not answered.

5. Projected costs of equipment needed for optimum operation are:
       Not answered.

Scholarships

The following undergraduate scholarships and graduate fellowships, teaching and otherwise, are awarded annually:

	Undergraduate		Graduate		Combination undergraduate and graduate	
	Number	Amount	Number	Amount	Number	Amount
Dance	2	$1,400	*	$ 2,500		
Music					66†	$25,520
Theater			*	13,500	*	8,850
Visual arts	*	1,000	*	9,800		
TOTAL		$2,400		$25,800		$34,379

* Varies.
† Figure approximate.

Qualitative Considerations

1. *a.* Is creative work considered equivalent to research in other disciplines as a criterion for promotion?
   Yes.
   b. Is an advanced academic degree required for appointment to the regular faculty?
   No.

2. Is there a growing question of the efficacy of tenure for faculty in the arts?
   No.

3. Effectiveness of the departments (faculty) in the following areas is felt to be:
   a. Contribution of new works in performance and exhibits: moderately
   b. Development of an increasingly sophisticated laity (audience): very effective
   c. Exploration of contemporary trends (arts movements):   moderately
   d. Vital, stimulating exploration of the heritage of each of the arts to introduce the seminal forces of the past: (not answered)
   e. Seeking new relationships in the arts: (not answered)

4. Do you feel your program is having any appreciable effect on the content and procedures of education in the arts in the schools—kindergarten through twelfth grade—in your state?

    No.

5. Admission for undergraduates in the arts is made:

    By the university admissions in consultation with the college and/or the departments.

6. A student major may be dropped from the college or department:

    A department may submit the name of a student to the dean if the faculty feels the student cannot profitably continue the major. The faculty must state the basis for their opinion and the probable cause of lack of success. The dean may permit change of major or, with approval of the president, require the student to withdraw.

7. Admission to graduate work is made:

    By the graduate college.

8. Impact on the surrounding community by student and faculty artists is felt to be:

    Strong.

9. Are you satisfied with your contribution to the number of "successful" working artists?

    Have no accurate information.

Arts Events

1. Are you provided with funds in the budget over and above any box office returns to produce arts events?

    Yes.

2. Is the college and/or departments directly involved in the cultural events presented by off-campus artists:

    a. By having ex officio members on the "cultural presentations" committee?

    Yes.

    b. By directly relating these events to curricular work?

    No.

UNIVERSITY OF CALIFORNIA AT SANTA CRUZ

The developments at Santa Cruz, just underway—writing began in 1965, music and visual arts in 1966, and dance, film, and theater in 1969—are interesting both because the campus is in a "start-up" stage and because of the cluster-college nature of the university's physical and administrative design. Also, last year over half of Santa Cruz's entering freshmen had a 4.0 average. Inspired by the English university system of separate colleges, the cluster colleges at Santa Cruz, which are set in a redwood forest, focus on different kinds of activities. College V is the cluster college in which the arts and the aesthetic education program reside. The Performing Arts Building was completed in the fall of 1971. But along with this centralization, there is a healthy effort to disperse interest in the arts throughout all the colleges, with student participation in each. In just three years, the number of music majors in the formal program has grown from 15 to 68, and the number of majors in visual arts has grown from 10 to 107. Theater began with 15 majors in 1971. Class enrollments in all arts have about doubled in three years. Officials feel that the first reasonable assessment of the program can be made in about three more years. Innovations at Santa Cruz are among the important experimental developments in the arts[4] that deserve continued attention.

UNIVERSITY OF CALIFORNIA AT SANTA CRUZ

Administration

1. Year institution of higher education founded: 1965.

2. Boards of studies in the arts formed:

Music	1966
Visual arts	1966
Dance	1969
Film	1969
Theater	1969

---

[4] Also very important to watch is the State University of New York, which has perhaps the greatest potential in the arts, academically and socially, of any state system of higher education. An assessment in five years of the developments underway there should prove extremely profitable.

3. Experimental administrative structure.

4. Administrative structure based on: tradition and careful design.

Student Personnel

1. Numbers of majors enrolled in the arts were:

Undergraduates	1971	1970	1969
Music	68	35	15
Theater	15		
Visual arts	107	23	10
TOTALS	190	58	25
No graduate students			

2. Total numbers of class enrollments of all students (nonmajors and majors) in all classes in the fall term were:

Undergraduates	1971	1970	1969	1968	1967
Music	227	87	113	88	51
Theater	220	235	178		
Visual arts	672	372	284	595	88
TOTALS	1,119	694	575	683	139

No graduate students

NOTE: Some arts courses are offered with the assistance of teaching assistants in the history of consciousness program. Writing courses are included in the board of studies in literature.

Faculty Personnel

	Sum of all FTE's
Music	6.2
Theater	5.5
Visual arts	10.5
TOTAL	22.2

Budget, 1970–71

	Amount of budget	*Percentage for salaries*	*Percentage for operating expenses*
Music	$ 89,249	78	22
Theater	88,554	70	30
Visual arts	111,134	85	15
TOTAL	$288,937	78	22

Space and Equipment

1. The capital investment in buildings for the arts is:
   $3,840,000.

2. The number of square feet for specialized studio and laboratory use (other than general classroom space) is:

Music	10,208
Theater	25,716
Visual arts	15,133
TOTAL	51,057

3. The present plant is effective for current artistic endeavor.

4. Capital investment for special equipment is:
   $12,000.

5. Projected costs of equipment needed for optimum operation are:

Music	$17,700
Theater	8,797
Visual arts	2,850
TOTAL	$29,347

Scholarships

There are no special scholarships for the arts. It is not presently known how many general undergraduate scholarships were awarded to students in the arts.

Qualitative Considerations

1. *a.* Is creative work considered equivalent to research in other disciplines as a criterion for promotion?
   Yes.
   b. Is an advanced academic degree required for appointment to the regular faculty?
   Yes. Ph.D., with the exception of visual arts.

2. Is there a growing question of the efficacy of tenure for faculty in the arts at your university?
   No.

3. Effectiveness of boards of studies (faculty) in the following areas is felt to be:
   a. Contribution of new works in performance and exhibits: not enough to moderately—there is always room for improvement
   b. Development of an increasingly sophisticated laity (audience): not enough to moderately
   c. Exploration of contemporary trends (arts movements): not enough to moderately
   d. Vital, stimulating exploration of the heritage of each of the arts to introduce the seminal forces of the past: not enough to moderately
   e. Seeking new relationships in the arts: not enough to moderately

4. Do you feel your program is having any appreciable effect on the content and procedures of education in the arts in the schools—kindergarten through twelfth grade—in your state?
   No. It is too soon to judge.

5. Admission for undergraduates in the arts is determined:
   By the university admissions in consultation with the college.

6. A student major may be dropped from the program:
   Because of lack of talent and/or performance without necessarily referring to grades.

7. Impact on the surrounding community by student and faculty artists is felt to be:
   Medium.

8. Are you satisfied with your contribution to the number of "successful" working artists?

"Pleased" perhaps, but not "satisfied." The program here is still quite young.

Arts Events

1. Are you provided with funds in the budget over and above any box office returns to produce arts events?

    No.

2. Are the arts directly involved in the cultural events presented by off-campus artists:
    a. By having ex officio members on the "cultural presentations" committee?

        Yes.
    b. By directly relating these events to curricular work?

        Yes for all arts.

3. Total number of arts events (all arts) from off-campus for which tickets are sold:

    8–10.

    Total admissions to arts events from off-campus: 5,000

    Total income from arts events from off-campus: $15,000

    Total expenses for arts events from off-campus: $16,000

Although there is a Division of Fine Arts at the University of Georgia, the departments within it — visual arts, drama and theater, and music — are virtually independent entities, all of which were established in 1932. One of the departments, visual arts, was selected by the board of regents and the president of the university as one of four areas of excellence to build toward eminence.

Architecture as such is not offered on this campus but is offered at Georgia Tech. Environmental design, however, is offered in visual arts. There is activity in film but not in the curriculum. Photographic design is offered in visual arts, and courses in various types of photography have developed in other parts of the university.

Although there has been substantial growth in the three departments, the penetration of the arts into the rest of the campus that has occurred in other institutions reported here has apparently not occurred at the University of Georgia.

UNIVERSITY OF GEORGIA

Administration

1. Year institution of higher education founded: 1785.

2. Departments in the arts formed:

Music	1932
Theater	1932
Visual arts	1932

3. There is a Division of Fine Arts within the College of Arts and Sciences. The chairman of this division reports to the dean of the college.

4. Present administrative structure due to: careful design.

Student Personnel

1. Numbers of majors enrolled in the arts were:

Undergraduates*	1971	1970	1969
Music	640†	535†	493†
Theater	98	84	75
Visual arts	665	564	532
TOTALS	1,403	1,183	1,100
Graduates	1971	1970	1969
Music	51	66	46
Theater	70	68	46
Visual arts	76	71	66
TOTALS	197	205	158

* Approximately 50 percent of undergraduate degree candidates are transfers from two-year institutions both within and without the university system of Georgia.
† Close estimate. No firm records are available.

2. Total numbers of class enrollments of all students (nonmajors and majors) in all classes in the fall term were:

Undergraduates	1971	1970	1969	1968	1967	1966
Music*	2,312	2,075	1,893	1,930	1,730	1,635
Theater	514	353	362	377		
Visual arts	2,434	2,317	2,106	2,328	2,098	1,816
TOTALS	5,260	4,745	4,361	4,635	3,828	3,451
Graduates	1971	1970	1969	1968	1967	1966
Music*	102	132	92	86	75	71
Theater	70	68	46	31	29	28
Visual arts	152	133	132	145	131	113
TOTALS	324	333	270	262	235	212

* Music class enrollment figures include band students and private lesson students.

NOTES: All enrollments are usually higher in the spring term than in the fall term.

Architecture as such is not offered, but environmental design and interior design are offered in visual arts.

Dance, in a very limited way, is offered by the department of physical education.

There is no program in film, but six or seven units of the university offer various types of courses in photography. Photographic design is offered in visual arts.

Creative writing has been offered in the past by the English department in a limited fashion, but there are presently negligible offerings in this area.

Faculty Personnel

	Number of full-time faculty FTE	Number of part-time faculty (bodies)	Sum of all FTE's	Number of student teaching assistants
Music	*	*	*	*
Theater	15			
Visual arts	50	2.83†	52.83	.50
TOTALS	65	2.83	52.83	.50

* Not reported. *The University of Georgia Bulletin, 1971–1973* lists 33 faculty members in music.
† FTE.

Budget, 1970–71

The sum of the budgets of the departments in the arts for the year 1970–71 was:

$1,849,121. Of this amount, $923,127 was budgeted for visual arts. Budget breakdown for the other two departments was not indicated.

Allocation in department budgets for salaries and operating expenses was:

	Percentage for salaries	Percentage for operating expenses
Music	85.00	15.00
Theater	90.00	10.00
Visual arts	95.29	4.71

Space and Equipment

1. The capital investment in buildings for departments in the arts is:
    $2,000,000.

2. The number of square feet for specialized studio and laboratory use (other than general classroom space) is:
    Estimated at 50,000.

3. Additional square feet needed:
    Music: 50,000.   Visual arts: 60,000.

4. Capital investment for special equipment is:
    $400,000 in visual arts.

5. Projected costs of equipment needed for optimum operation are:

Music	$ 85,000
Theater	30,000
Visual arts	75,000
TOTAL	$190,000

Scholarships

The following graduate fellowships, teaching and otherwise, are awarded annually:

	Number	*Total amount in dollars*
Visual arts	20	$43,924

Qualitative Considerations

1. *a.* Is creative work considered equivalent to research in other disciplines as a criterion for promotion?
   Yes.
   b. Is an advanced academic degree required for appointment to the regular faculty?
   Yes.

2. Is there a growing question of the efficacy of tenure for faculty in the arts?
   Yes, to a slight degree.

3. Effectiveness of the departments (faculty) in the following areas is felt to be:
   a. Contribution of new works in performance and exhibits: moderately
   b. Development of an increasingly sophisticated laity (audience): moderately
   c. Exploration of contemporary trends (arts movements):   moderately
   d. Vital, stimulating exploration of the heritage of each of the arts to introduce the seminal forces of the past: moderately
   e. Seeking new relationships in the arts: not enough

4. Do you feel your program is having any appreciable effect on the content and procedures of education in the arts in the schools—kindergarten through twelfth grade—in your state?
   Yes. Our graduates carry into the school systems the emphasis on arts education, not arts education.

5. Admission for undergraduates in the arts is made:
   Response unclear.

6. A student major may be dropped from the department:
   Because of lack of talent and/or performance or because of grades below a certain point.

7. Admission to graduate work is made:
   With auditions and/or portfolio, and by the graduate college with recommendation from the department.

8. Impact on the surrounding community by student and faculty artists is felt to be:
   Strong in visual arts.

9. Are you satisifed with your contribution to the number of "successful" working artists?
   Faculty: Yes.   Student: Yes.

Arts Events

1. Are you provided with funds in the budget over and above any box office returns to produce arts events?
   No.

2. Are the departments directly involved in the cultural events presented by off-campus artists:
   a. By having ex officio members on the "cultural presentations" committee?
   No.
   b. By directly relating these events to curricular work?
   Not answered.

3. Total number of arts events (all arts) from off-campus for which tickets are sold:
   18–25.

   Total admissions to arts events from off-campus: Data not available.

   Total income from arts events from off-campus: Data not available.

   Total expenses for arts events from off-campus: Data not available.

4. Estimates of the percentage breakdown of attendance between *(a)* students and faculty and *(b)* the community at major on-campus events of the following type are:

	Student/Faculty (percent)	Community (percent)
Music	60	40
Theater	50	50
Visual arts	60	40

Support for the arts has been strong at the University of New Mexico since its beginning in 1889, and the College of Fine Arts was formed at a relatively early date, 1936. Currently student demand for enrollment in arts courses far exceeds available and usable space. The increase in the numbers of majors, including majors in dance (in the music department) and in film (in theater), is great enough for the college to be seeking a limit on enrollments. Class enrollments in dance went from a beginning of 42 in 1970 to 78 the following year. Class enrollments in film, introduced in 1968, increased from 156 to 473 in 1971. This is the sort of response experienced all over the country to the introduction of dance and film.

The Tamarind Institute, a center for research and development in printmaking which receives outside support, was moved from Los Angeles to the university in 1970. This is an example of a university campus becoming a haven for professional work and research in the arts.

The growth of the arts at the University of New Mexico, as in many other Western and Midwestern institutions of higher education, may perhaps be due to the fact that it was unfettered by the traditional emphasis on critical scholarship as opposed to creative work that is found in much of the East and the South (excluding Florida). In any case, resistance to the arts—the making of art as distinct from the collecting, criticizing, and writing of history— appears to be much more prevalent in the East and South than in the Midwest and the West. The University of New Mexico provides an example of a well-organized, comprehensive, and growing program in the arts, especially with its recent developments in theater, dance, and film.[5]

UNIVERSITY OF NEW MEXICO

Administration

1. Year institution of higher education founded: 1889.

2. Departments in the arts formed:

[5] To the north, the University of Utah, undoubtedly because of the strong tradition in the state left as a heritage of Brigham Young, has long been a bulwark for the arts in the West and is currently providing national leadership in dance.

Visual arts	1897
Music	1898
Architecture	1936
Theater	1936
Dance (courses)	1962
Tamarind Institute	1970

3. College of Fine Arts established in 1936. The dean of this college reports to the vice-president of academic affairs.

4. Present administrative structure is due to: historical chance and careful design.

Student Personnel

1. Numbers of majors enrolled in the arts were:

*Undergraduates**	*1971*	*1970*	*1969*
Architecture	300	260	200
Music	230	230	200
Theater	100	110	100
Visual arts	630	525	450
TOTAL	1,260	1,125	950

Graduates	*1971*	*1970*	*1969*
Architecture	64	37	20
Music	16	17	23
Visual arts†	79	103	70
TOTAL	159	157	113

*Figures on undergraduate majors enrolled are approximate, since freshmen and sophomores enrolled in University College are not required to declare majors until they transfer to the College of Fine Arts.

† Graduate enrollment in visual arts was deliberately cut back in 1971, as it had outreached space and faculty in 1970. A graduate enrollment of two or three times greater would exist except for deliberate limitation.

2. Total numbers of class enrollments of all students (nonmajors and majors) in the fall term were:

Undergraduates and graduates*	1971	1970	1969	1968	1967	1966
Architecture	1,332	868	654	521	517	411
Music	2,816	2,300	1,788	1,837	2,002	1,876
Theater	717	556	501	477	392	412
Visual arts	3,382	3,208	2,508	2,224	2,085	2,054
Dance†	78	42				
Film‡	473	427	216	156		
TOTAL	8,798	7,401	5,667	5,215	4,996	4,753

*Undergraduate and graduate class enrollments are reported together, since the university course numbering system makes it impossible clearly to separate such enrollments.

† Dance courses are in the music department.

‡ Film courses are in the theater department.

NOTE: Class enrollments in all areas would have risen even more sharply than they did had space been available to meet the demand.

Faculty Personnel

	Number of full-time faculty FTE	Number of part-time faculty (bodies)	Sum of all FTE's	Number of student teaching assistants
Architecture	6	8	9.17	5
Music	22	11	26.40	4
Theater	7	1	7.17	
Visual arts	25	11	30.00	21
Dance	1	1	1.33	
Film		1	.67	1
TOTAL	61	33	74.74	31

Budget, 1970–71

	Amount of budget	Percentage for salaries	Percentage for operating expenses
Architecture	$ 143,150	96.3	3.7
Music*	350,975	94.2	5.8
Theater†	108,850	90.7	9.3
Visual arts	413,600	96.9	3.1
Sum of departments	$1,016,575	94.7	5.3
Administrative office	74,750	71.4	28.6
Art museum	42,500	70.0	30.0
Part-time instruction	36,000		
Summer school	51,500		
Tamarind Institute	18,600		
TOTAL	$1,239.925		

*Includes dance.
†Includes film.

Space and Equipment

1. The capital investment for total College of Fine Arts buildings is:

Music	$3,065,000*
Theater	51,300†
Visual arts	165,000‡
Tamarind Institute	80,000
TOTAL	$3,361,300

*Includes the total Fine Arts Center, but not Popejoy Concert Hall. The Fine Arts Center includes an art museum, art history classrooms, fine arts library, etc. The cost of these spaces cannot be separated from music.
† Does not include space temporarily in use as a theater.
‡ Construction cost in the 1920s.
  NOTE: These figures are badly distorted by inflation.

2. The number of square feet for specialized studio and laboratory use (other than general classroom space) is:

Architecture	11,100
Music	26,000
Theater	9,000
Visual arts	26,500
Dance	3,600
Tamarind Institute	4,600
TOTAL	80,800

NOTE: Construction on a new theater building, with 28,800 square feet net usable space will start in the spring of 1972. Construction on a new art building, now in programming phase and funded for $3,000,000, will begin in 1973.

3. Is the present plant effective for current artistic endeavor?
   Yes: Music, art museum.　　　No: Other fields.
   Additional square feet needed:
   Minimum of 128,000.

4. Capital investment in special equipment is:

Architecture	$ 26,500
Music	296,900
Theater	25,200
Visual arts	50,000
Art museum	29,000
Fine arts library	26,600
Tamarind Institute	28,000
TOTAL	$482,200

NOTE: These figures are distorted by inflation.

5. Projected costs of equipment needed for optimum operation are:

Music	$175,000
Theater	*
Visual arts	*

* Will be included in construction budget for new building.

Scholarships

The following undergraduate scholarships and graduate fellowships, teaching and otherwise, are awarded annually:

	Number of undergraduate scholarships	Total amount in dollars	Number of graduate fellowships	Total amount in dollars
Architecture	8	$ 2,600	5.0	$12,000
Music	67	16,215	6.0	14,000
Theater	1	25		
Visual arts	1	450	25.5	56,900
College			3.0	7,200
TOTALS	77	$19,290	39.5	$90,100

Qualitative Considerations

1. *a.* Is creative work considered equivalent to research in other disciplines as a criterion for promotion?
      Yes.
   b. Is an advanced academic degree required for appointment to the regular faculty?
      No.

2. Is there a growing question of the efficacy of tenure for faculty in the arts?
      Yes, particularly in the creative fields.

3. Effectiveness of the departments (faculty) in the following areas is felt to be:
   a. Contribution of new works in performance and exhibits: very effective in exhibitions; not enough in performances
   b. Development of an increasingly sophisticated laity (audience): very effective in music; moderately in visual arts; not enough in theater and dance
   c. Exploration of contemporary trends (arts movements): very effective in visual arts; not enough in dance, music, and theater
   d. Vital, stimulating exploration of the heritage of each of the arts to introduce the seminal forces of the past: very effective in art history; moderately in music; not enough in art museum (limitations of funds make it difficult to exhibit enough "old art")
   e. Seeking new relationships in the arts: not answered—felt question unclear

4. Do you feel your program is having any appreciable effect on the content and procedures of education in the arts in the schools—kindergarten through twelfth grade—in your state?
      Not much. The arts seem to be losing some ground in the public

schools due to budgetary pressures. New Mexico programs in the visual arts have never been strong.

5. Admission for undergraduates in the arts is made:
    By the university admissions in consultation with the college.

6. A student major may be dropped from the college or department:
    Because of lack of talent and/or performance or because of grades below a certain point.

7. Admission to graduate work is made:
    By the graduate college with recommendation from the departments.

8. Impact on the surrounding community by student and faculty artists is felt to be:
    Medium.

9. Are you satisfied with your contribution to the number of "successful" working artists?
    Faculty: Yes, except for theater.   Student: Yes, except for theater.

Arts Events

1. Are you provided with funds in the budget over and above any box office returns to produce arts events?
    Yes.
    The budgets for this purpose annually amount to:

College	$ 3,000*
Architecture	1,500
Music (including dance)	14,000
Theater	6,000
Visual arts	8,500
TOTAL	$33,000

*For visiting lecturers.

2. Is the college and/or the departments directly involved in the cultural events presented by off-campus artists:
    a. By having ex officio members on the "cultural presentations" committee?
    Yes.

    b. By directly relating these events to curricular work?

Architecture	No
Music	If yes, only in a very limited way
Theater	If yes, only in a very limited way
Dance	If yes, only in a very limited way
Film	If yes, only in a very limited way
Visual arts	Yes

3. Total number of arts events (all arts) from off-campus for which tickets are sold:

        28 (not including rock concerts).

Total admissions to arts events from off-campus: Approximately 45,000

Total income from arts events from off-campus: $153,000

Total expenses for arts events from off-campus: $141,000

4. Estimates of the percentage breakdown of attendance between *(a)* students and faculty and *(b)* the community at major on-campus events of the following type are:

	Student/Faculty (percent)	*Community (percent)*
Architecture	70	30
Dance	50	50
Music	50	50
Theater	50	50
Visual arts (art museum)	67	33

NOTE: These are intuitive estimates in the absence of figures.

Students

Everyone would like to understand students today—or think he does. Remembering that each individual is just that and will act like himself, taxonomy not withstanding, I perceive that students in the arts fall into five groups. There are (1) the students who know they want to play the cello or sculpt or act or choreograph or design buildings or make movies or write stories and poetry. They have made a commitment to themselves and to the arts they are pursuing, and they are readily identifiable. Then there are (2) the students who are shopping, seeking to define their interests. Students in this category fall into two subgroups: those who are aware of their quest and the excitement and enjoyment of pursuing it and those who are virtually at sea and sadly couldn't see land if it were dead ahead. Another group—a fairly new and growing one—is composed of (3) those who are taking a major in one of the arts just because they like it and want to get a college education by that route. This is a time-honored practice by which students have majored, for example, in economics, political science, history, English, or French to get a degree before going into business or marriage. This group, at least in such increasing numbers, is relatively new to the arts. ("Serious" students in the thirties would seldom have taken a major in the arts when respectable majors in "solid" subjects were available!) Another group is composed of (4) those in other majors who take courses in the arts because they like them. Their style of life includes the arts and that's all there is to it. This is also a growing number. (At one university the most imaginative, skillful, and disciplined potter is a graduate student in physics.) There is also (5) a kind of fifth column of floaters. With slight or great talent, they are usually well-designed in dress and personality and exhibit great commitment and assurance, but they don't seem to finish much. Bizarre events thwart them, and some are accident prone.[6] They are often more visible to the campus than students in the previous four categories because they are seldom in the study, in the studio, or at rehearsal.

Whether careful study would reveal that these five categories exist in any valid and reliable way, I don't know; but many teachers and administrators in the arts report that these divisions, which are based on observation, are useful to them. There are, of course,

---

[6] They tend to have difficult interpersonal relationships, to drop tools on their feet, to be attacked for style of dress or hair, etc.

many crossovers, dropouts, and identity crises among these five categories. In any case, the bulk of students are extremely attractive, reasonably talented, committed young people who know how to work and are using higher education well.

But what will they do when they graduate? A marketing approach to this question comes up with a pretty grim outlook. Most institutions are careful to indicate to their students the overwhelming odds against making a living as a professional artist. After this reality check, they encourage those who feel a real commitment to one or more of the arts to see if they can "make it." Society would be the poorer if such students did not have the opportunity to try. Some opt for teaching. Some simply use their training as a sound general education background. And some switch fields quite successfully. The country surely needs a manpower survey in the arts and its related fields.[7] With such information, students would know the odds they are facing and could determine options available to them as alternates to a livelihood as a professional artist. Since it is extremely hazardous to predict success or failure among the talented and industrious, it is prudent rather than callous for student advisors to declare the difficulties and leave the decision of pursuing the arts up to the student. In any case, it is incumbent upon every school to institute a *professional* follow-up program for its graduates and its dropouts.

Resistance to and support for the rise of the arts in academe
Discernible from the histories of the growth of the arts in academe is the resistance of early Protestant ethics and the depersonalization of the industrial-technological revolution.[8] These forces were expressed rationally and irrationally, but the arts didn't go away. Here and there, on either side of the turn of the twentieth century, a strong personality would carve a niche for himself by introducing

[7] A complementary switch to the emergence of women in the professions is noted in the report of a percentage increase of men over women in the arts at two-year colleges. Percentage changes in the numbers of new enrollees in the arts in two-year colleges, public and private, in 1971 show an 11.6 percent increase for men and a 0.3 percent increase for women (Peterson, 1972, p. 26). If women can invade "male strongholds," men can invade "female strongholds."

[8] Depersonalization here refers to man living to suit the machine rather than vice-versa. Such phenomena as students being summarized on an IBM card ("Don't fold, crumble or spindle!"), the "dehumanizing" of workers on an assembly line, homogenizing food, and packaged meals, living in fear of a "computerized life," and "Muzak" are current examples.

a course or two. What repeated itself, according to the best of anecdotal reports of this process, was the protection, support, leadership, understanding, drive, concern, and/or interest of an administrator, often the president of the university. I believe that a careful study of the growth of the arts on individual campuses will support this idea. At UCLA a series of chancellors was aggressively supportive: Clarence A. Dykstra saw the new department of theater arts into being, Vern Knudsen encouraged the growth and building program of the College of Fine Arts, and Franklin Murphy did the same with a special concern for dance. Herman Wells' leadership and encouragement of the arts at Indiana University, particularly of music with a heavy accent on opera, is unabated as this is written after almost 40 years. President Dickey at Dartmouth took a personal hand in guiding the development of the Hopkins Art Center. Clark Kerr, during his presidency, initiated the statewide University of California Creative Arts Fund from his office. This is to say that an administrator is in a position to clear the way for the arts to move and can interpret the values of the arts to recalcitrant deans in the other disciplines, committees of the faculty, trustees, and state legislators. I think the arts would still be peripheral on many more campuses than they are today if it weren't for the aggressive support of top administrators.[9]

Resistance to the arts often appears to come first from the general faculty. Anything new is a threat to the status quo and a drain on funds and attention in the eyes of this group, most of whom have been raised on a diet of discursive symbols in their professional lives. With Plato, they simply reject the artist as a serious member of their company. Amusing entertainments and "sings" are all fine as extracurricular displays of adolescent animal spirits, but they are unwilling to accept an artist as a colleague.[10]

[9] Herman Wells told the author of a theory of administration in which the president always backs something that seems absolutely exotic. Years later, what seemed exotic is seen as a solid, forthright beginning.

[10] Today many colleges and universities are fissioning off the arts into administrative units of their own. The University of Maryland, the University of Hawaii, and Hofstra University are current examples. (Over half of the arts units represented in the International Council of Fine Arts Deans came into being after 1961.) Often this fissioning has been done with general campuswide support, but sometimes groups of faculty have been determined not to let the mickey mice have their own club. Some of the arts faculty themselves have not been convinced that they were ready to stand on their own artistic method, based on the discipline arising from the perception and invention of nondiscursive symbols, and have counseled against leaving the womb of "arts and sciences."

Although some faculty members don't agree, most arts administrators across the country find strong support from the scientists. Most artists and scientists "dig" each other. Perhaps the imagination, risk, rigor, and reality demanded by scientific study is similar to that of the "artistic method." In any case, both sooner or later must lay their works on the line, and this may account for much of the support for the arts from scientists.

The 17 reporting institutions of this study indicated relatively few outright negative stands against the arts on their campuses and generally rated the following components of the campus community as very supportive, supportive, or mildly supportive to negative:[11]

Very supportive	*Supportive*	*Mildly supportive-negative*
Chief executive	Board of trustees	Vice-president of business affairs
Student body	Chief officer of academic affairs	
Alumni in the arts		Student government
Local community	Academic senate	Engineering and technology faculty
National private foundations	University curriculum council	
		Professional schools
	Humanities faculty	College of education
	Social science faculty	Buildings and grounds
	Science and math faculty	State legislature
		Federal agencies
	Alumni association	Corporations
	Campus business office	Business and merchants
	Alumni (general)	Idiosyncratic nature of artists-teachers
	State and local private foundations	
	Arts organizations	
	Collegiality of faculty	

Of the above, only federal agencies failed to get at least one of the highest ratings of support from any school. Only two categories received the lowest possible rating from a school: state and local private foundations and the dean of a college in which the arts are located.

When a strong administrator has been present—a dean or vice-president of academic affairs, a chancellor or a president—the arts have had a better chance to stand on their own feet.

[11] Appendix A is a scattergram showing all ratings on a scale from −5 to +5.

A particularly interesting point of view about boards of trustees or regents was reflected in these ratings. According to this view, other fields have trustees who share their special interests, but there is seldom a champion for the arts among the trustees. Advocates of the arts on the board might help persuade their fellow trustees—who should not be considered to have antiarts positions—to go along with increased support for the arts.

In general, then, the arts are in favor on the campuses of the country and are getting stronger; but there are still pockets of resistance—some of the older artist-teachers themselves, a traditional or even reactionary group of faculty, some state legislators—and there are fractures of collegiality due to status quo or austerity budgets. [12] Resistance to the expansion of the arts—all the arts, not just art and music—remains rather strong in some places. Some faculty in other departments seem to feel that the arts should be present on the campus, but should hang their clothes on a hickory limb and not go near the water. The arts are so expensive, it is claimed.

Accordingly, those on campuses who wish to bring the arts into full play in academe should develop solid and aggressive support within the arts; astute leadership; the support of someone high in the administrative hierarchy; the support of faculty in the other disciplines (particularly the sciences); and a clear, practical, and progressive program. Thus armed, they should enter the lists to compete for the budget dollar and studio space. Such efforts can be successful.

Rate of change in the rise of the arts
After 250 years of peripheral activity around the campus and occasional sorties into sacred ground, the arts began to achieve small beachheads on the shores of academe by the turn of the twentieth century. Between the two world wars, the arts became clearly established in the curriculum, but they were a relatively weak force in campus affairs. They were interesting, occasionally diverting or entertaining, nice appurtenances which could be embarrassing, but which were, in any case, not substantial and rarely serious. After World War II, however, there was a sharp

[12] On an austerity budget for fiscal 1973, Ohio University proposes an increase for the College of Fine Arts and decreases for the Colleges of Engineering and Education.

acceleration in growth which became substantial.[13] In the present era of status quo or austerity budgets, growth of programs and facilities has slowed somewhat, but student interest and enrollment have not. Projections to 1980–81 based on national norms indicate continuing growth in the arts about as great as the increase in the number of young people entering college. This estimate may be too conservative. Some administrators feel that the rate of growth of the last 15 years reflects not a fad or a phase of interest that will level off but a trend that will continue and increase. My own estimate is that the rate of growth in the arts in higher education will exceed the normal growth in higher education as a whole. The numbers of majors in the arts may level off or decline slightly, but class enrollments should go up at an above normal rate of growth. If I am right, allocation of funds for faculty, space, and equipment for the arts will be a significant problem that must be met throughout the country during the seventies.

[13] According to the author's study for the International Council of Fine Arts Deans in 1971, four of the fifty-six institutions reporting had established administrative units in the arts (colleges, schools, or divisions) before 1900; one between 1900 and 1920; six between 1920 and 1930; six between 1930 and 1940; two between 1940 and 1950; two between 1950 and 1960; and thirty after 1960.

5. Recommendations

In working with the information in this report and the people who provided it, I came to the conclusion that colleges and universities should consider the following recommendations:

1 A shabby laissez-faire view of *all* the arts on campus (architecture, dance, film, music, theater, poetry, and visual arts) is no longer possible morally, intellectually, or aesthetically. Therefore, each responsible institution in higher education should take a stand in its policy for the teaching, studying, and making of the arts in that institution—whatever that stand may be.

2 Departments, schools, and colleges of the arts can no longer afford a pristine isolation from the rest of the campus and/or community (local, regional, national, and international). Therefore, they should each develop a comprehensive program with a two-pronged approach, one emphasizing the student major and the arts per se and the other emphasizing general education—the nonmajor, teacher training, and the community.

3 The arts on campus tend to be subject to the worst of academic ills. Compartmentalization and parochialism abound where mutual concern should prevail. (Perhaps the greatest reward in academic life is true collegiality.) Therefore, departments, colleges, and schools of the arts should deliberately learn to know and to understand their colleagues both within and without their departments to further their own work and the work of others within the university.

4 It is clear that "bigger" is not necessarily "better" in student body size. A golden mean or optimum number of majors in each of the arts is not only highly desirable but necessary. There can be too few to make up a performing group or too many to get into the avail-

able space, let alone to get an education. Even more important is the consideration that collegiality among students is more easily arrived at with an appropriate student body size in each of the arts. Therefore, each department should determine its most effective size and, by interviewing, portfolios, and auditions before matriculation and careful counseling after, keep each student body at an optimum size for the development of student artists.

5   On campus and off, questions are raised about what students do who graduate in the arts—Can they make a living at it? Therefore, each institution should establish a professional follow-up study of its graduates and dropouts.

6   It is reported that few trustees or regents are appointed who have backgrounds in the arts. Therefore, we recommend that one or more trustees or regents for each institution be appointed because of background or special interest in the arts.

7   Change is so rapid today that some established departments in the arts are bogged down, especially where the average age of the faculty is close to retirement. Accordingly, the following criteria are offered for use in self-assessment and self-study:

a.   Development of new works, performance and exhibition of new works, new artists, new artist-teachers, and new architect-planners.

b.   Development of an increasingly sophisticated laity as audience (an informed, sensitive, active citizenry), aware of its environment from an aesthetic as well as practical and technical point of view.

c.   Exploration of the contemporary movements in the arts and the environment, as well as exploration of society's current response to the arts in all segments of socioeconomic scale and ethnic background

d.   A vitalized and stimulating exploration of the heritage of each of the arts with an emphasis on introducing to the immediate scene the seminal forces of the past

e.   Search for new relationships among the arts with increased flexibility in each of the departments

f.   Search for the optimum number of graduate students and undergraduates in each school or program in terms of its mission

g. Development of university-based "R&D centers" or "institutes" to provide opportunity for total, professional application to problems in the arts

h. Development of further funds through advisory boards for the arts

8 Scientists learn about "grantsmanship" and proposal writing before they are out of graduate school. Indeed, many owe their support for graduate work to "soft money" from sources outside the university. Artists in the university, however, have not had this experience and, generally speaking, are unsophisticated about seeking financial support from the public or the private sectors (Chagy, 1971). And their administrators reflect this lack of sophistication, except in relatively rare cases like the UCLA Arts Council—although the council supports only the visual arts rather than the arts across the board. Of the institutions included in this study, less than half have a formal organization, a friends of the arts, for example, to promote outside funds. We recommend, then, that each administrative unit representing the arts on each campus formally set up an organization to provide information on likely sources of funds, to guide preparation of proposals, and to seek individual and collective donors. Special interests in a given art or artist can be preserved by tagging such gifts, though these benefactors may also be encouraged to give undesignated funds.

9 Teaching in the arts from nursery school through continuing education, with some brilliant exceptions, is generally ineffective and even destructive in some cases. Therefore, under the auspices of an appropriate national body such as the American Council on Education, the American Council for the Arts in Education, or a major national foundation, a commission for reordering the teaching of the arts should be created. Similarly, on each campus a president's committee to study teacher education in the arts should be established with universitywide membership to report findings and recommendations to the president.

10 With dance, song, and ritual, architecture is among the oldest of the arts, but it suffers the most from today's ills of scale and the consequent socioeconomic problems of the city and the country. Special attention is needed. Therefore, a task force should be commissioned to seek and preserve the aesthetic components in architecture and planning as they relate to the other arts and to the curriculum at all levels.

11   With the growth of the arts and the unusual number of students going into the area—most of them studying a field far different from that which their fathers studied—students in the arts appear to be noticeably different from those of any previous generation. Society as well as admissions and guidance officers, let alone the faculty in the arts, needs to know more about these students. Therefore, we recommend that a causal-comparative study of graduates and dropouts in all the arts be made on a national basis.

12   Universities should explore the possibility of providing for the arts, particularly for the performing arts, something analogous to the "R&D center" or "institute" developed after World War II for science, medicine, technology, and a few scholarly pursuits. It has been observed that there is a "mismatch between the social ethos of the university and the social ethos of the institute: the one is individual and democratic, the other collective and hierarchical" (Orlans, 1972, p. 167). Because of the basic nature of their endeavors, dance, film, theater, music, and architecture could be well served by the collective and hierarchical ethos of the institute. And it is possible that such an institute could also serve the visual arts in their current forms as they break into and penetrate the other arts, technology, and political action. *All* the arts in the country today desperately need opportunities to make their statements at reduced expense, without the restrictions and academic restraints universities hold, and should hold, so dear. What is needed is the bringing together of first-rate artists with the opportunity to make artistic discoveries at their own rate, by letting one thing lead to another. And the institute idea does permit flexibility in arrangements, since the institute need not be established in a permanent setup with personnel and space on a year-round basis.

Because of the failure of the universities to provide such opportunity for the theater, young and committed artists created off-Broadway and, later, off-off-Broadway. Jerome Robbins' Workshop, funded by the National Arts Endowment and the endowment's grants to top choreographers for new works, is evidence that such "R&D" efforts produce just that—new works. The summer workshops for dance at Connecticut College over the years, as well as the present efforts of the Eugene O'Neill Foundation's playwrights' workshop in the summer, are other examples of this type of endeavor. While it lasted, the UCLA Theater Group was a productive "institute."

Since the rise of the arts on campus is due, if my interpretation is correct, to students and faculty simply insisting on activities in the arts, it is no wonder that most departments in universities are still performance-oriented. They should continue to be so, but not to the extent that often is the case today when student artists are veritably thrust into performance for the public. Most of the leading professional training programs for actors have now forbidden public performance by their actors for one to three years.[1] While students are developing their art in the studio, moreover, there is more opportunity to develop means, such as institutes, by which valuable buildings and equipment can be used by professionals to the benefit of the university and the artistic community alike. The failure to develop such cooperative use of facilities now allows some excellent plants to lie idle for periods from as long as May to October.

Many obstacles—such as union problems, possessive faculties, and fears of being "commercial"—lie in the way of the development of "R&D centers" for the arts on campuses, but I submit that the time for developing new works under less costly and more conducive conditions is here and that more movement in this direction will allow the emergence of new leadership in the field. The arts on the campus need to be "professionalized," and they need a better climate and a greater number of opportunities for artists to work. Harold Orlans (1972) has clearly presented the dangers and promises of such ventures. It remains to be seen who in the various universities, especially in those near urban centers which are loaded with unused talent, will put together talent, time, space, and money in a way that will create productive institutes for the arts. In any case, the successful institutes in other areas, like the Rand Corporation, the Rockefeller Institute (now Rockefeller University), and the Brookings Institution should be used as analogs, not templates.

---

[1] After three years, the first acting class of the new drama school at Juilliard made its first public appearance in June 1971, to great critical acclaim. Carnegie-Mellon and NYU, among others, have done the same. Rigorous training in the studio with an "in-house" audience has taken the place of "putting on a play," which was the initial force in campus theater.

References

American Federation of Arts: *American Art Directory,* compiled by the Jacques Cattell Press, Inc., R. R. Bowker Company, New York, 1970.

Anderson, Joseph: Untitled notes, Ohio University, Athens, 1972.

Association of College and University Concert Managers: *Profile Survey III,* analyzed by Robert Moon, 1970. (Mimeographed.)

Atkinson, J. Edward (ed.): *Black Dimensions in Contemporary American Art,* New American Library, New York, 1971.

Bell, Daniel: "The Cultural Contradictions of Capitalism," *The Journal of Aesthetic Education,* vol. 6, nos. 1–2, pp. 11–38, January–April 1972; originally published in the *Public Interest,* no. 21, pp. 16–44, Fall 1970.

Bloom, Kathryn: "Development of Arts and Humanities Program," in *Toward an Aesthetic Education,* pp. 89–101, a report of an institute sponsored by CEMREL, Inc., Music Educators National Conference, Washington, 1971.

Boas, Frederick S.: *University Drama in the Tudor Age,* Oxford, 1914.

Chagy, Gideon (ed.): *The State of the Arts and Corporate Support,* Paul S. Eriksson, Inc., New York, 1971.

The Chronicle of Higher Education, April 17, 1972.

College Art Association of America: *The Visual Arts in Higher Education,* a study (Andrew C. Ritchie, director) prepared under a grant from the Ford Foundation, New Haven, Conn., 1966.

Council on Higher Education in the American Republics: *The Arts and the University,* Institute of International Education, New York, 1964.

Dance: A Projection for the Future, The Developmental Conference on Dance, University of California, Los Angeles, Nov. 24–Dec. 3, 1966, and May 28–June 3, 1967, Impulse Publications, Inc., San Francisco, 1968.

Graham, Kenneth L. (ed.): "The Relationships Between Educational Theatre and Professional Theatre: Actor Training in the U.S.," *Educational Theatre Journal,* November 1966.

Harvard University: *Report of the Committee on the Visual Arts at Harvard University,* John Nicolas Brown, chairman, Cambridge, Mass., 1956.

Langer, Susanne K.: "The Cultural Importance of the Arts," lecture delivered at Syracuse University, reprinted in *Philosophical Sketches,* Mentor Books, New American Library, Inc., New York, 1964; originally published in Michael F. Andrews (ed.), *Aesthetic Form and Education,* Syracuse University Press, Syracuse, N.Y., 1958.

Lewis, Anthony: "To Grow and to Die: III," *New York Times,* Feb. 5, 1972, op-ed page.

Madden, Dorothy: Untitled manuscript, University of Maryland, College Park, 1972.

Mahoney, Margaret (ed.): *The Arts on Campus: The Necessity for Change,* New York Graphic Society, Greenwich, Conn., 1970.

Marks, Joseph E., III: *America Learns to Dance,* Exposition Press, New York, 1957.

Matthews, Albert: "Early Plays at Harvard," *Nation,* vol. 98, March 19, 1914.

Meltz, Noah M.: *Patterns of University Graduations by Field of Study in Ontario, Canada and the United States, 1950–51 to 1968–69,* Institute for Policy Analysis, University of Toronto, Toronto, July 1971a.

Meltz, Noah M.: *Projections of University Graduations by Field of Study in Ontario, Canada and the United States, 1969–70 to 1980–81,* Institute for Policy Analysis, University of Toronto, Toronto, August 1971b.

Monroe, Charles R.: *Profile of the Community College,* Jossey-Bass, San Francisco, 1972.

Morrison, Jack: "The Arts as Early Warning Signals," *Arts in Society,* vol. 8, no. 2, pp. 469–477, Nov. 2, 1971.

National Center for Educational Statistics: *A Taxonomy of Instructional Programs in Higher Education,* U.S. Office of Education, Washington, 1970a.

National Center for Educational Statistics: *Earned Degrees Conferred: 1969–1970 Institutional Data,* U.S. Office of Education, Washington, 1970b.

Orlans, Harold: *The Nonprofit Research Institute: Its Origin, Operation, Problems, and Prospects,* McGraw-Hill Book Company, New York, 1972.

Perkins, James A.: "The University and the Arts," *T. C. Record,* pp. 671–678, May 1965.

Peterson, Richard E.: *American College and University Enrollment Trends in 1971,* Carnegie Commission on Higher Education, Berkeley, Calif., 1972.

Quincy, Josiah: *History of Harvard University,* Boston, vol. I, 1860.

Rice, Norman L.: Untitled manuscript, Carnegie-Mellon University, Pittsburgh, Pa., 1972.

Seaborg, Glenn T.: "The Government-University Partnership in Graduate Education," *The Graduate School Faces Current Problems,* Conference on Graduate Schools in the United States, Proceedings of the Eighth Annual Meeting, San Francisco, Dec. 4–6, 1968, pp. 28–46. (Reprinted by the Educational Resources Information Center, ERIC #ED 030 364.)

Stillings, Frank S.: Untitled manuscript, Central Michigan University, Mount Pleasant, 1972.

U.S. Office of Education: *Museums and Related Institutions: A Basic Program Survey,* Bureau of Research, Washington, 1969.

Wallace, Karl R. (ed.): *A History of Speech Education in America: Background Studies,* Appleton Century Crofts, New York, 1954.

Weatherhead, Arthur C.: *The History of Collegiate Education in Architecture in the United States,* a Columbia University doctoral dissertation, published by the author, Los Angeles, 1941.

Wright, Charles D.: "A Survey of the Creative Writing and Writer-in-Residence Programs," Proceedings of the Sixth National Conference on the Arts in Education, National Council of the Arts in Education, Pennsylvania State University, University Park, 1967.

Appendix A: Resistance to or Support for the Rise of the Arts: Ratings from Reporting Institutions

FIGURE A-1
Resistance or support ratings from reporting institutions

	Board of trustees	Chief executive	Chief officer of academic affairs	Vice-President of business affairs	Dean of the college in which arts reside	Academic senate	Student government
Support +5	••••	••••• •	••••• •••	•••	••••• •••••	••	•
+4	•	••••	•	•	•	•••	•
+3	•••	•••	•••	••••	•	•••••	•••••
+2	•••		•	•		•	••
+1		•	•	•	•		
0	••••		•	•••••	•	•••	••••• •
−1		•					
−2						•	
−3							
−4							
Resistance −5					•		

Student body at large	University curriculum council	Humanities disciplines	Social sciences disciplines	Science and math disciplines	Engineering and technology	Professional schools	School (college) of education	Alumni association
•••	•	••••		•	•	•	•	••
••••	•••	••••	••••	•••		••	••	••••
••••• •	•••••	••	••••	•••	•		••	••
	•	•••	••	••	•••	••	•••	•
•	•	••	••	•	•			•
•	••••		••	•••••	••••• ••••	••••• •••••	••••• ••	••••• •
			•					

**Figure A–1
(continued)**

	Campus business office	Buildings and grounds	Alumni (general)	Alumni in the arts	Local community	State legislature	Federal agencies
Support +5	•	•	••	••••• •	•••••	•	
+4	•••	••	•••	•••••	••••		•
+3	••••	••		•	••	••	•••
+2	•	•	••••	•	•	••	•••
+1		••	•••	•	••	••	••
0	••••• •	•••••	•••	•	•	••••• ••	••••• •
−1		•					
−2							
−3		•				•	
−4							
Resistance −5							

Private state and local foundations	*Private national foundations*	*Corporations*	*Business and merchants*	*Arts organizations*	*Idiosyncratic nature of artists and teachers*	*Collegiality of faculty*	*Other, affiliates*	*Other state art council*	*Other, local press*
●●	●●●		●●	●●	●●	●●●			
●	●●●●	●		●	●●	●●			
●●●	●●●	●●	●●	●●●●● ●	●	●●	●		●
●●●	●●	●●●	●		●●	●			
●●	●	●	●●●	●					
●●		●●●●● ●	●●●●●	●●●●●	●●●●● ●●	●●●●● ● ●●			
●	●●	●	●		●				
		●			●				
			●						
								●	
●									

Appendix B: Earned Degrees Conferred in the Arts, 1967-68, 1968-69, and 1969-70

TABLE B-1 Bachelor's, master's, and doctor's degrees conferred in institutions of higher education, by sex of student, control of institution, and area of study: aggregate United States, 1967–68, 1968–69, 1969–70

	Bachelor's degree requiring four or five years			Master's degree			Doctor's degree		
	Total	Men	Women	Total	Men	Women	Total	Men	Women
Architecture									
All 1967-68	2,956	2,830	126	536	509	27	6	6	
All 1968-69	3,331	3,188	143	579	542	37	7	6	1
All 1969-70	3,902	3,698	204	658	615	43	11	10	1
Public 1967-68	2,250	2,164	86	214	202	12	1	1	
Public 1968-69	2,598	2,501	97	234	224	10	6	6	
Private 1967-68	706	666	40	322	307	15	6	6	
Private 1968-69	733	587	46	345	318	27	6	5	
Fine and Applied Arts									
All 1967-68	25,555	10,403	15,152	6,563	3,704	2,859	528	428	100
All 1968-69	31,640	12,950	18,690	7,414	4,094	3,320	684	565	119
All 1969-70	35,945	15,361	20,584	7,849	4,158	3,691	734	592	142
Public 1967-68	14,395	6,015	8,380	4,231	2,400	1,831	330	280	50
Public 1968-69	18,083	7,548	10,535	4,832	2,731	2,101	438	375	63
Private 1967-68	11,160	4,388	6,772	2,332	1,304	1,028	198	148	50
Private 1968-69	13,557	5,402	8,155	2,582	1,363	1,219	246	190	56

SOURCE: National Center for Educational Statistics: *Earned Degrees Conferred, 1967–68, 1968–69, 1969–70*, U.S. Office of Education, Washington, 1969, 1970, 1971.

TABLE B-2 *Bachelor's, master's and doctor's degrees conferred in institutions of higher education, by sex of student and fields of study: aggregate United States, 1967–68, 1968–69, 1969–70*

	Bachelor's degree requiring four or five years			Master's degree			Doctor's degree		
	Total	Men	Women	Total	Men	Women	Total	Men	Women
Fine and Applied Arts									
Arts general									
1967–68	7,121	2,278	4,843	1,341	804	537	24	18	6
1968–69	9,321	2,991	6,330	1,442	815	627	21	18	3
1969–70	10,598	3,594	7,004	1,523	867	656	18	12	6
Music, including sacred music									
1967–68	4,173	1,818	2,355	1,898	1,078	820	185	158	27
1968–69	5,021	2,145	2,876	2,040	1,123	917	255	216	39
1969–70	5,433	2,424	3,009	2,130	1,128	1,002	278	237	41
Speech and dramatic arts									
1967–68	7,331	2,984	4,347	2,071	1,032	1,039	269	219	50
1968–69	8,825	3,664	5,161	2,342	1,181	1,161	299	250	49
1969–70	10,367	4,604	5,763	2,546	1,194	1,352	301	256	45
Fine and applied arts, all other fields									
1967–68	6,930	3,323	3,607	1,253	790	463	50	33	17
1968–69	8,473	4,150	4,323	1,590	975	615	109	81	28
1969–70	9,547	4,739	4,808	1,650	969	681	137	87	50

TABLE B-2 *(continued)*

	Bachelor's degree requiring four or five years			Master's degree			Doctor's degree		
	Total	*Men*	*Women*	*Total*	*Men*	*Women*	*Total*	*Men*	*Women*
Art Education									
1967–68	4,460	1,233	3,227	832	340	492	35	23	12
1968–69	4,720	1,346	3,374	942	361	581	32	22	10
1969–70	5,504	1,503	4,001	1,047	406	641	40	28	12
Music Education									
1967–68	6,464	2,747	3,717	1,581	925	656	81	72	9
1968–69	7,100	3,052	4,048	1,682	953	729	92	81	11
1969–70	7,353	3,190	4,163	1,606	838	768	90	81	9

SOURCE: National Center for Educational Statistics: *Earned Degrees Conferred, 1967-68, 1968-69, 1969-70,* U.S. Office of Education, 1969, 1970, 1971.

Appendix C: Educational Data on the Arts in the United States

TABLE C-1 *Enrollment in institutions of higher education, by sex and by type and control of institution: United States and outlying areas, fall 1960 and fall 1965*

	Number of students, 1960			Number of students, 1965			Percentage change, 1960–1965		
	Total	Men	Women	Total	Men	Women	Total	Men	Women
Total, public and private									
All institutions	3,610,007	2,270,640	1,339,367	5,570,271	3,396,574	2,173,697	+54.3	+49.6	+62.3
Two-year institutions	453,617	283,292	170,325	845,244	523,532	321,712	+86.3	+84.8	+88.9
Four-year institutions	3,156,390	1,987,348	1,169,042	4,725,027	2,873,042	1,851,985	+49.7	+44.6	+58.4
Schools of art*	15,166	8,241	6,925	21,119	10,328	10,791	+39.3	+25.3	+55.8
Public									
All institutions	2,135,690	1,326,545	809,145	3,654,578	2,205,652	1,448,926	+71.1	+66.3	+79.1
Two-year institutions	393,553	253,565	139,988	739,918	466,019	273,899	+88.0	+83.8	+95.7
Four-year institutions	1,742,137	1,072,980	669,157	2,914,660	1,739,633	1,175,027	+67.3	+62.1	+75.6
Schools of art*	257	130	127	790	315	475	+207.4	+142.3	+274.0
Private									
All institutions	1,474,317	944,095	530,222	1,915,683	1,190,922	724,771	+29.9	+26.1	+36.7
Two-year institutions	60,064	29,727	30,337	105,326	57,513	47,813	+75.4	+93.5	+57.6
Four-year institutions	1,414,253	914,368	499,885	1,810,367	1,133,409	676,958	+28.0	+24.0	+35.4
Schools of art*	14,909	8,111	6,798	20,329	10,013	10,316	+36.4	+23.4	+51.8

*Emphasizing painting, sculpture, and design, but including drama, music, dance, etc.

SOURCE: National Center for Educational Statistics: *Digest of Educational Statistics, 1970,* U.S. Office of Education, Washington, 1970.

TABLE C-2 Enrollment for advanced degrees, by sex of student and by field of study: United States and outlying areas, fall 1969

	Enrollment in fall 1969			Percentage change 1968–1969		
	Total	*Men*	*Women*	*Total*	*Men*	*Women*
Enrollment for master's and doctor's degrees	756,865	492,599	264,266	+ 7.5	+ 5.1	+12.5
Architecture	1,948	1,708	240	+36.8	+35.8	*
Fine and applied arts	26,614	14,133	12,481	+11.0	+ 9.8	+12.4

* Percentage change reported only if 1968 enrollment was 500 or more.

SOURCE: National Center for Educational Statistics: *Digest of Educational Statistics. 1970.* U.S. Office of Education, Washington, 1970.

TABLE C-3 Professional background and academic activity of college faculty members, by type of institution and by sex: United States, spring 1969 (percentage distribution)

	All institutions			Universities			Four-year colleges			Two-year colleges		
	Total	*Men*	*Women*	*Total*	*Men*	*Women*	*Total*	*Men*	*Women*	*Total*	*Men*	*Women*
Major field of postgraduate degree												
Fine Arts	6.3	6.0	7.6	5.1	4.8	6.7	8.0	7.7	9.1	6.5	6.8	5.7

SOURCE: National Center for Educational Statistics: *Digest of Educational Statistics, 1970.* U.S. Office of Education, Washington, 1970.

Appendix D: National Norms Relating to the Arts for Entering College Freshmen

TABLE D-1   *Weighted national norms for all freshmen*

	All institutions	All two-year colleges	All four-year colleges	All universities
*Father's occupation**				
Artist (including) performer				
Fall 1970	0.9	0.8	0.8	1.0
Fall 1971	0.8	0.7	0.8	0.9
Probable major field of study				
Fine arts				
Fall 1966	8.4	8.7	8.2	8.4
Fall 1970	9.2	9.4	8.5	9.9
Fall 1971	9.0	8.1	9.2	10.1
Probable career occupation				
Artist (including) performer				
Fall 1966	6.6	6.8	6.2	7.0
Fall 1970	6.2	5.9	5.7	7.3
Fall 1971	6.0	4.7	6.6	7.1
Objectives considered to be essential or very important				
Achieve in a performing art				
Fall 1966	10.8	9.6	11.6	10.7
Fall 1970	12.8	11.5	13.5	13.5
Fall 1971	11.9	9.7	13.7	12.7
Create works of arts				
Fall 1966	15.1	15.2	14.9	15.4
Fall 1970	16.2	15.2	16.3	17.6
Fall 1971	15.4	13.8	15.7	17.6
Percentage of students reporting that during the past year they				
Played a musical instrument				
Fall 1966	51.4	44.2	54.6	52.3
Fall 1970	38.5	32.9	41.0	42.3
Fall 1971	37.7	32.2	40.5	42.5

Two-year colleges		Four-year colleges					Universities	
Public	Private	Technical institutions	Public	Private nonsect.	Protestant	Catholic	Public	Private
0.9	0.5	0.5	0.7	1.2	0.9	1.0	1.0	1.1
0.7	0.8	0.7	0.6	1.3	0.9	0.8	0.9	1.2
8.8	8.3	3.3	7.6	7.3	9.7	8.6	8.4	8.6
9.1	10.7	2.6	8.0	10.9	10.5	7.5	10.0	9.9
7.6	12.4	3.9	8.8	11.8	11.7	7.4	10.7	7.9
6.9	6.3	1.1	5.2	7.3	6.8	7.5	6.7	7.8
5.5	7.7	0.3	5.3	8.6	6.6	5.8	7.0	7.9
4.4	7.9	2.3	6.0	9.6	7.8	6.2	7.4	6.0
9.6	9.7	6.4	10.2	13.7	13.2	11.7	10.4	11.7
11.1	12.8	7.7	12.6	17.4	15.0	13.9	12.9	14.9
9.4	13.0	7.5	12.6	17.8	16.6	13.2	11.9	15.3
15.5	13.9	8.7	13.4	16.8	15.2	17.4	15.1	16.5
14.7	17.0	7.8	15.7	21.2	16.6	16.7	17.8	16.9
13.4	17.2	9.7	14.8	20.4	17.1	15.8	18.0	16.4
42.8	49.9	45.8	49.9	56.6	63.2	53.4	51.6	54.7
31.5	37.9	37.8	38.0	46.3	47.6	39.2	41.0	45.2
31.9	35.0	36.1	37.7	45.5	47.8	38.2	41.2	47.3

TABLE D-1 *(continued)*

	All institutions	All two-year colleges	All four-year colleges	All universities
Read poetry not required in course*				
Fall 1970	57.2	50.2	60.7	61.0
Fall 1971	59.3	52.2	64.2	63.1
Visited art gallery or museum*				
Fall 1970	68.8	64.8	70.6	71.4
Fall 1971	66.2	61.5	67.5	71.8

*Item not included in 1966 survey.

SOURCE: American Council on Education: *The American Freshman: National Norms for Fall 1966, Fall 1970, Fall 1971,* Washington, 1966, 1970, 1971.

Two-year colleges		Four-year colleges					Universities	
Public	*Private*	*Technical institutions*	*Public*	*Private nonsect.*	*Protestant*	*Catholic*	*Public*	*Private*
48.2	57.6	44.9	59.7	67.4	63.4	62.2	60.4	62.5
51.3	61.2	50.4	63.7	69.2	67.4	65.6	62.3	65.8
64.0	67.8	65.7	69.5	75.3	71.1	71.4	69.7	75.1
61.1	65.1	64.0	64.6	74.2	70.2	70.0	70.4	77.1

Appendix E: Data on the American Graduate Student Relating to the Arts

TABLE E-1 *Percentage distribution of American graduate students among academic disciplines, by sex*

	Intended major field as entering freshman			Actual undergraduate major		
	Male	*Female*	*Total*	*Male*	*Female*	*Total*
Architecture and/or design	1.0	0.2	0.7	0.5	0.2	0.4
Fine Arts	0.1	0.2	0.1	0.1	0.2	0.2
Art	0.5	2.2	1.0	0.6	2.3	1.2
Dramatics	0.2	1.4	0.6	0.2	1.0	0.5
Speech	0.3	1.3	0.7	0.5	1.0	0.7
Music	1.5	3.3	2.1	1.5	2.6	1.9
Other fine arts	0.1	0.2	0.2	0.2	0.2	0.2

SOURCE: American Council on Education: *The American Graduate Student: A Normative Description,* Washington, 1971.

TABLE E-2 *Attitudes of American graduate students toward higher education and their academic experience and highest degree expected (percentage distribution)*

	All groups combined			Ph.D.		
	Male	*Female*	*Total*	*Male*	*Female*	*Total*
Need for firm undergraduate background in arts and music						
Extremely important	9.5	20.3	13.2	10.2	23.0	13.4
Fairly important	26.0	44.8	32.4	25.8	37.2	28.6
Fairly unimportant	42.6	26.9	37.2	40.1	30.4	37.7
Extremely unimportant	21.9	7.9	17.2	23.9	9.4	20.3

SOURCE: American Council on Education: *The American Graduate Student: A Normative Description,* Washington, 1971.

Current graduate department			Field of master's (actual or intended)			Field of doctorate (actual or intended)		
Male	*Female*	*Total*	*Male*	*Female*	*Total*	*Male*	*Female*	*Total*
0.5	0.2	0.4	0.6	0.2	0.4	0.2	0.1	0.2
0.1	0.3	0.2	0.1	0.2	0.2	0.3	0.4	0.3
0.5	1.7	0.9	0.1	0.2	0.2	0.3	0.4	0.3
0.3	0.9	0.5	0.4	0.9	0.6	0.4	1.4	0.6
0.4	1.5	0.8	0.5	1.6	0.9	0.4	1.2	0.6
1.3	2.1	1.5	1.5	2.2	1.8	1.4	1.9	1.5
0.2	0.3	0.2	0.2	0.5	0.3	0.2	0.3	0.2

Highest degree expected								
Ed.D., D.A., and other			*First professional*			*Subdoctoral, nonprofessional*		
Male	*Female*	*Total*	*Male*	*Female*	*Total*	*Male*	*Female*	*Total*
12.8	21.9	15.9	6.4	12.2	7.6	7.6	17.3	12.4
27.8	45.2	33.8	26.9	37.4	29.1	22.1	51.1	36.4
47.2	25.8	39.8	46.2	35.3	43.9	44.1	25.1	34.7
12.2	7.1	10.4	20.5	15.1	19.4	26.2	6.6	16.5

Table E-3 *Demographic and background characteristics of American graduate students, by sex and highest degree expected (percentage distribution)*

	All groups combined			Ph.D.		
	Male	*Female*	*Total*	*Male*	*Female*	*Total*
Attend a concert						
Once a week or more	1.1	1.3	1.1	1.5	1.6	1.5
Two or three times a month	3.9	5.4	4.4	4.2	7.5	5.0
About once a month	11.7	15.9	13.2	13.7	19.2	15.1
A few times a year	43.2	49.9	45.5	44.2	52.2	46.2
Once a year or less	40.1	27.5	35.8	36.4	19.5	32.2
Attend an "art" film						
Once a week or more	1.5	2.1	1.7	1.9	2.1	1.9
Two or three times a month	5.9	7.8	6.5	7.3	11.1	8.2
About once a month	14.8	17.1	15.6	17.0	23.3	18.6
A few times a year	32.4	34.5	33.1	34.5	38.2	35.4
Once a year or less	45.5	38.5	43.1	39.3	25.2	35.9
Attend a play						
Once a week or more	0.4	0.3	0.4	0.4	0.5	0.4
Two or three times a month	2.2	4.1	2.8	2.5	5.6	3.2
About once a month	12.1	18.2	14.2	13.4	21.4	15.4
A few times a year	49.7	55.5	51.7	48.3	53.7	49.7
Once a year or less	35.7	21.8	30.9	35.5	18.9	31.4
Attend an art exhibition						
Once a week or more	0.8	1.4	1.0	0.7	1.9	1.0
Two or three times a month	2.9	5.1	3.6	3.2	6.3	3.9
About once a month	11.1	15.7	12.7	13.5	20.0	15.2
A few times a year	42.5	49.9	45.1	44.9	50.9	46.4
Once a year or less	42.7	27.9	37.6	37.6	20.9	33.5

SOURCE: American Council on Education: *The American Graduate Student: A Normative Description,* Washington, 1971.

| Highest degree earned | | | | | | | | |
| Ed.D., D.A. and other | | | First professional | | | Subdoctoral, nonprofessional | | |
Male	Female	Total	Male	Female	Total	Male	Female	Total
1.8	1.9	1.8	0.3	0.7	0.4	0.7	1.2	0.9
8.2	6.5	7.6	3.0	5.4	3.5	1.6	3.6	2.6
11.6	16.9	13.4	12.2	19.2	13.7	7.1	12.9	10.0
40.5	51.9	44.4	46.2	47.0	46.3	39.5	48.9	44.2
37.9	22.7	32.8	38.4	27.7	36.1	51.1	33.4	42.3
0.8	2.3	1.3	1.2	1.6	1.3	0.9	2.1	1.5
4.6	9.1	6.1	4.9	7.4	5.4	3.2	5.7	4.4
11.3	12.8	11.8	16.9	19.0	17.4	10.5	11.9	11.2
31.7	38.2	33.9	35.5	39.4	36.4	27.5	31.9	29.7
51.6	37.6	46.8	41.4	32.5	30.6	57.9	40.5	53.2
0.4	0.6	0.5	0.4	0.3	0.4	0.3	0.1	0.2
2.5	5.1	3.4	2.1	3.3	2.3	1.5	3.5	2.5
10.4	19.5	13.5	11.4	18.6	13.0	9.0	14.4	11.7
52.3	57.1	53.9	52.2	60.0	53.9	50.6	57.6	54.1
34.4	17.7	28.7	33.9	17.8	30.4	38.6	24.4	31.5
0.7	1.7	1.0	0.8	0.5	0.7	0.9	1.0	0.9
3.7	5.5	4.3	2.8	3.0	2.8	1.5	4.1	2.8
9.9	15.2	11.7	9.1	15.0	10.4	8.3	13.1	10.7
40.4	53.2	44.8	45.1	52.4	46.7	36.8	49.5	43.2
45.3	24.4	38.2	42.2	29.1	39.5	52.4	32.3	42.3

	Biosciences	*Business*	*Education*
Attend a concert			
Once a week or more	0.5	0.4	0.4
Two or three times a month	3.7	1.8	4.3
About once a month	12.1	9.0	10.1
A few times a year	42.0	44.6	45.5
Once a year or less	41.7	44.2	39.6
Attend an "art" film			
Once a week or more	0.8	0.9	1.0
Two or three times a month	5.1	3.0	4.6
About once a month	12.8	11.1	10.3
A few times a year	31.6	33.4	30.5
Once a year or less	49.8	51.6	53.5
Attend a play			
Once a week or more	0.2	0.4	0.2
Two or three times a month	1.3	2.1	2.9
About once a month	8.0	13.8	13.4
A few times a year	45.7	51.0	53.8
Once a year or less	44.8	32.6	29.7
Attend an art exhibition			
Once a week or more	0.4	0.6	0.6
Two or three times a month	2.1	1.8	3.2
About once a month	11.4	9.2	10.7
A few times a year	43.5	41.9	44.1
Once a year or less	42.7	46.5	41.5

SOURCE: American Council on Education: *The American Graduate Student: A Normative Description,* Washington, 1971.

Engineering	Arts and humanities	Mathematics and physical sciences	Social sciences	Health fields	Law
0.5	3.9	1.3	0.6	0.1	0.2
3.0	8.1	4.6	3.9	4.2	3.0
10.3	19.2	14.1	14.0	13.6	14.2
41.7	46.5	42.2	50.7	47.2	48.5
44.5	22.3	37.8	30.9	34.9	34.1
0.8	4.3	1.4	1.9	0.1	1.1
4.4	11.7	5.3	9.5	3.3	6.5
11.9	24.2	15.2	20.8	8.8	20.6
30.5	34.6	32.4	36.8	30.3	37.8
52.4	25.2	45.7	31.0	57.5	34.0
0.3	0.9	0.2	0.2	0.0	0.2
1.5	5.6	2.2	2.9	1.5	2.5
10.2	19.5	10.0	17.8	10.0	15.9
45.7	53.5	48.2	52.7	50.5	54.8
42.3	20.5	39.5	26.5	38.0	26.5
0.6	3.0	0.3	0.7	0.4	0.8
1.9	6.7	2.5	4.9	2.3	3.5
9.8	19.1	11.2	14.3	7.0	13.1
39.0	48.3	43.6	49.9	45.2	49.3
48.6	23.0	42.5	30.3	45.1	33.3

Appendix F: Questionnaire Used for This Study

Official: _____

Institution: _____

Address: _____

A PROFILE OF EDUCATION IN THE ARTS IN
INSTITUTIONS OF HIGHER EDUCATION

(This information may be identified with the university and reported to the Carnegie Commission on Higher Education. _____)

Please initial

1. a. Year the institution of higher education was founded: _____
   b. Year the first department concerned with the arts was formed:
      art _____, music _____, other _____, other _____
   c. If the arts are in a college, school, division, or other unit of the arts, that unit was formed in the year of _____. The name of the unit is_____.
   d. What college or other unit are the arts in? (Please specify)
      _____
   e. The following departments were formed in the years of:
      architecture _____, dance _____, film _____, music _____, theatre _____, writing _____, visual arts _____, other _____.

2. The arts in this institution are in one administrative unit.
   Yes _____ No _____

3. a. Numbers of majors enrolled in the arts were:

Student Majors Enrolled

	Undergraduate			Graduate		
	1971	1970	1969	1971	1970	1969
Architecture						
Dance						
Film						
Music						
Theater						
Writing						
Visual arts						
Other						
Other						
TOTAL						

Comment on growth: _____

b. In the last five years enrollment has been:
   (1) up, same, down for majors
   (2) up, same, down for class enrollments
   Please comment: _____

c. The total numbers of class enrollments of all students (nonmajors and majors) in all classes in the fall quarter (or semester) were:

Undergraduates

	1971	1970	1969	1968	1967	1966
Architecture						
Dance						
Film						
Music						
Theater						
Writing						
Visual arts						
Other						
Other						

Graduates

	1971	1970	1969	1968	1967	1966
Architecture						
Dance						
Film						
Music						
Theater						
Writing						
Visual arts						
Other						
Other						

  d. Have you developed the optimal enrollment of majors for each of the arts? Yes _____ No _____

  e. Do you hold to that enrollment? Yes _____ No _____
   Comment: _____
   _____

4. The units in the college are known as (please circle):
  departments, schools, divisions, other _____

5. The head of each unit is called (please circle):
  chairman, director, head, other _____

6. If there is a dean or director (chief officer for the arts), he reports to: president, vice-president of academic affairs, dean of faculties, provost, other _____

7. a. In the administrative hierarchy of power, budget, and space the arts are:
   (1) in a respected position _____
   (2) so-so _____
   (3) barely tolerated _____
   (4) threatened _____
   (5) on the way out _____
   Please describe: _____
   _____

  b. The arts have risen rapidly on campus over the last 20 years. There has been good support for this rise and there has also been some resistance. This question attempts to identify both support and resistance. If you think the question is not significant or is obscure, circle "0." If resistance has been severe in a given case, circle "5" on the resistance side of the scale; if support has been strong, circle "5" on the other side—or whatever seems appropriate, weak to strong, on the 0–5 scale.

Support for or Resistance to the Arts on Campus

Strong support   (Circle Appropriate Number)   *Strong Resistance*

The board of trustees (or regents, etc.)

5 4 3 2 1 0 1 2 3 4 5

The chief executive (president, chancellor)

5 4 3 2 1 0 1 2 3 4 5

Chief officer of academic affairs

5 4 3 2 1 0 1 2 3 4 5

Vice-president of business affairs

5 4 3 2 1 0 1 2 3 4 5

Dean of college in which the arts reside

5 4 3 2 1 0 1 2 3 4 5

Academic senate (or other faculty body)

5 4 3 2 1 0 1 2 3 4 5

Student government

5 4 3 2 1 0 1 2 3 4 5

Student body at large

5 4 3 2 1 0 1 2 3 4 5

University curriculum council (if not, please name _____)

5 4 3 2 1 0 1 2 3 4 5

Humanities disciplines

5 4 3 2 1 0 1 2 3 4 5

Social science disciplines

5 4 3 2 1 0 1 2 3 4 5

Science and math disciplines

5 4 3 2 1 0 1 2 3 4 5

Engineering and technology

5 4 3 2 1 0 1 2 3 4 5

Professional schools (law and medicine)

5 4 3 2 1 0 1 2 3 4 5

| *Strong support* | | | | | | | *School (college) of education* | | | | | | | | *Strong resistance* |

<table>
<tr><td colspan="11" align="center">School (college) of education</td></tr>
<tr><td>5</td><td>4</td><td>3</td><td>2</td><td>1</td><td>0</td><td>1</td><td>2</td><td>3</td><td>4</td><td>5</td></tr>
<tr><td colspan="11" align="center">Alumni association</td></tr>
<tr><td>5</td><td>4</td><td>3</td><td>2</td><td>1</td><td>0</td><td>1</td><td>2</td><td>3</td><td>4</td><td>5</td></tr>
<tr><td colspan="11" align="center">Campus business office (purchasing, accounting, etc.)</td></tr>
<tr><td>5</td><td>4</td><td>3</td><td>2</td><td>1</td><td>0</td><td>1</td><td>2</td><td>3</td><td>4</td><td>5</td></tr>
<tr><td colspan="11" align="center">Buildings and grounds (maintenance and custodial)</td></tr>
<tr><td>5</td><td>4</td><td>3</td><td>2</td><td>1</td><td>0</td><td>1</td><td>2</td><td>3</td><td>4</td><td>5</td></tr>
<tr><td colspan="11" align="center">Alumni (general)</td></tr>
<tr><td>5</td><td>4</td><td>3</td><td>2</td><td>1</td><td>0</td><td>1</td><td>2</td><td>3</td><td>4</td><td>5</td></tr>
<tr><td colspan="11" align="center">Alumni in the arts</td></tr>
<tr><td>5</td><td>4</td><td>3</td><td>2</td><td>1</td><td>0</td><td>1</td><td>2</td><td>3</td><td>4</td><td>5</td></tr>
<tr><td colspan="11" align="center">Local community</td></tr>
<tr><td>5</td><td>4</td><td>3</td><td>2</td><td>1</td><td>0</td><td>1</td><td>2</td><td>3</td><td>4</td><td>5</td></tr>
<tr><td colspan="11" align="center">State legislature</td></tr>
<tr><td>5</td><td>4</td><td>3</td><td>2</td><td>1</td><td>0</td><td>1</td><td>2</td><td>3</td><td>4</td><td>5</td></tr>
<tr><td colspan="11" align="center">Federal agencies</td></tr>
<tr><td>5</td><td>4</td><td>3</td><td>2</td><td>1</td><td>0</td><td>1</td><td>2</td><td>3</td><td>4</td><td>5</td></tr>
<tr><td colspan="11" align="center">Private, state and local foundations</td></tr>
<tr><td>5</td><td>4</td><td>3</td><td>2</td><td>1</td><td>0</td><td>1</td><td>2</td><td>3</td><td>4</td><td>5</td></tr>
<tr><td colspan="11" align="center">Private national foundations</td></tr>
<tr><td>5</td><td>4</td><td>3</td><td>2</td><td>1</td><td>0</td><td>1</td><td>2</td><td>3</td><td>4</td><td>5</td></tr>
<tr><td colspan="11" align="center">Corporations</td></tr>
<tr><td>5</td><td>4</td><td>3</td><td>2</td><td>1</td><td>0</td><td>1</td><td>2</td><td>3</td><td>4</td><td>5</td></tr>
<tr><td colspan="11" align="center">Business and merchants</td></tr>
<tr><td>5</td><td>4</td><td>3</td><td>2</td><td>1</td><td>0</td><td>1</td><td>2</td><td>3</td><td>4</td><td>5</td></tr>
<tr><td colspan="11" align="center">Arts organizations—commercial and industrial (e.g. graphics, film, TV, music, etc.)</td></tr>
<tr><td>5</td><td>4</td><td>3</td><td>2</td><td>1</td><td>0</td><td>1</td><td>2</td><td>3</td><td>4</td><td>5</td></tr>
<tr><td colspan="11" align="center">Idiosyncratic nature of artists-teachers</td></tr>
<tr><td>5</td><td>4</td><td>3</td><td>2</td><td>1</td><td>0</td><td>1</td><td>2</td><td>3</td><td>4</td><td>5</td></tr>
<tr><td colspan="11" align="center">Collegiality of faculty</td></tr>
<tr><td>5</td><td>4</td><td>3</td><td>2</td><td>1</td><td>0</td><td>1</td><td>2</td><td>3</td><td>4</td><td>5</td></tr>
<tr><td colspan="11" align="center">Other (describe)</td></tr>
<tr><td>5</td><td>4</td><td>3</td><td>2</td><td>1</td><td>0</td><td>1</td><td>2</td><td>3</td><td>4</td><td>5</td></tr>
<tr><td colspan="11" align="center">Other (describe)</td></tr>
<tr><td>5</td><td>4</td><td>3</td><td>2</td><td>1</td><td>0</td><td>1</td><td>2</td><td>3</td><td>4</td><td>5</td></tr>
</table>

8. a. Among the criteria for promotion in your university, is the creative work of your faculty considered equivalent to research in science, social science and the humanities?

   Yes _____ No _____

   b. Among the criteria for appointment to the regular faculty is an academic degree required? Yes _____ No _____; an advanced degree? Yes _____ No _____. If yes, what degree?

   _____

9. Admission for undergraduates to the college (and therefore one of its units) or departments in the arts is made:

   _____ a. by university admissions office without recourse to the college

   _____ b. by the university admissions in consultation with the college

   _____ c. by the college

   _____ d. by the college after admission to the university

   _____ e. with auditions and/or portfolio

   _____ f. other (please describe) _____

   _____

10. A student major may be dropped from the college or department:

    _____ a. because of lack of talent and/or performance without necessarily referring to grades

    _____ b. because of grades below a certain point

    _____ c. other (please describe) _____

    _____

11. a. Teacher preparation for kindergarten through twelfth grade is controlled:

    _____ (1) by the college or department

    _____ (2) by the college of education

    _____ (3) by the college or department and the college of education

    _____ (4) other (please describe) _____

    _____

    b. Teacher credentials are awarded after:

    (1) four years _____

    (2) five years _____

12. Recommendation for awarding of the degree is by:

    _____ a. the college and/or department

    _____ b. the college and university requirements

    _____ c. other (please describe) _____

    _____

13. Admission to graduate work is made:
    _____ a. by the graduate college
    _____ b. by the graduate college with recommendation from the college
    _____ c. by the college with recommendation to the graduate college
    _____ d. with auditions and/or portfolio
    _____ e. other (please describe) _____

14. a. The total college budget or the sum of the budgets of the departments in the arts for the year 1970-71 is: $ _____.
    b. The budgets for each of the various departments are:

    | Architecture | $ _____ | Theater | $ _____ |
    | Dance | $ _____ | Writing | $ _____ |
    | Film | $ _____ | Visual arts | $ _____ |
    | Music | $ _____ | Other | $ _____ |

    c. Of the total college budget or sum of the budgets of the departments _____% is for salaries and _____% for operating expenses.
    d. The percentages for salaries and operating expenses for each of the various departments are:

    | Architecture | _____% salaries | _____% operating expenses |
    | Dance | _____ % salaries | _____% operating expenses |
    | Film | _____% salaries | _____% operating expenses |
    | Music | _____% salaries | _____% operating expenses |
    | Theatre | _____% salaries | _____% operating expenses |
    | Writing | _____% salaries | _____% operating expenses |
    | Visual arts | _____% salaries | _____% operating expenses |
    | Other | _____% salaries | _____% operating expenses |

    e. The university (administration and faculty) understands the peculiar needs of the arts such as space, equipment, time, production funds:
    _____ (1) very well
    _____ (2) reasonably so
    _____ (3) in a vague way
    _____ (4) not at all
    _____ (5) in a hostile way

15. The budget is prepared:
    _____ a. by the dean
    _____ b. by the dean in consultation with the chairman of each unit
    _____ c. by the dean with the chairman in consultation with

the chairman of each unit and a faculty (faculty-student) budget committee.

_____ d.   other (please describe) _____

_____

16.   Budget hearings are held at the level of vice-president of academic affairs.

Yes _____No _____Other (please describe) _____

_____

_____

17.   a.   The capital investment for total college buildings or sum of departments in the arts is $ _____.

b.   The capital investments for each of the various departments are:

Architecture	$ _____	Theater	$ _____
Dance	$ _____	Writing	$ _____
Film	$ _____	Visual arts	$ _____
Music	$ _____	Other	$ _____

18.   a.   The total number of square feet for specialized studio and laboratory use (other than general classroom space) in the college or sum of the departments in the arts is _____.

b.   The total number of square feet for each of the various departments are:

Architecture	_____	Theater	_____
Dance	_____	Writing	_____
Film	_____	Visual arts	_____
Music	_____	Other	_____

c.   The present plant is effective for current artistic endeavor.

Yes _____   No _____

d.   We need _____ square feet renovated.

e.   We need _____ additional square feet.

f.   Please elaborate. _____

_____

19.   a.   Capital investment for special equipment for the college or sum of the departments in the arts is $ _____.

b.   Capital investments for special equipment for each of the various departments are:

Architecture	$ _____	Theater	$ _____
Dance	$ _____	Writing	$ _____
Film	$ _____	Visual arts	$ _____
Music	$ _____	Other	$ _____

c.   Needed equipment (not presently available) for optimum operation in the college or sum of the departments in the arts amounts to $ _____.

d. Needed equipment for optimum operation for each of the various departments amounts to:

Architecture $ _____   Theater $ _____

Dance $ _____   Writing $ _____

Film $ _____   Visual arts $ _____

Music $ _____   Other $ _____

20. Is your present administrative structure for the arts due to:
    a. tradition _____
    b. historical chance _____
    c. powerful personality _____
    d. careful design based on educational concept, principle, and function _____
    (Please explain) _____

    _____

21. Besides your regular gallery openings, concerts and productions, do you have a special program to bring the arts of the college or of the departments into the mainstream of campus life (dorms, student and faculty centers) by means of events, classes with or without credit, with student and faculty participation?
    Yes _____ No _____
    (Please describe) _____

    _____

22. Is the college and/or departments directly involved in the cultural events presented by off-campus artists:
    a. by ex officio members from the college on the "cultural presentations" committee?
        Yes _____ No _____
    b. by directly relating these events to curricular work?

        Architecture Yes _____ No _____

        Dance   Yes _____ No _____

        Film   Yes _____ No _____

        Music   Yes _____ No _____

        Theater   Yes _____ No _____

        Writing   Yes _____ No _____

        Visual arts   Yes _____ No _____

        Other _____ Yes _____ No _____
    c. Is the cultural program of off-campus artists strictly in the hands of extension services?
        Yes _____ No _____
        Explain _____

23. a. Do you feel you have an impact on the surrounding community (residents, schools, business, industry) with your student and faculty artists?

    Strong ————   Weak ————

    Medium ————   None ————

    Comment: ————————————————————

    b. What would you estimate the percentage of attendance is at major on-campus events of the following type:

	Student/Faculty	*Community*
Architecture	%	%
Dance	%	%
Film	%	%
Music	%	%
Theater	%	%
Writing	%	%
Visual arts	%	%
Other	%	%

    c. Through a formal organization (Friends of the Arts, etc.), do you receive financial support from the community?

        College   Yes ———— No ————

        Architecture Yes ———— No ————

        Dance   Yes ———— No ————

        Film   Yes ———— No ————

        Music   Yes ———— No ————

        Theater   Yes ———— No ————

        Writing   Yes ———— No ————

        Visual arts   Yes ———— No ————

        Other   Yes ———— No ————

    d. Do you receive outside financial support for the college and the departments from:

        State arts council   Yes ———— No ————

        City arts council   Yes ———— No ————

        Foundations   Yes ———— No ————

        Individual donors   Yes ———— No ————

        Alumni association   Yes ———— No ————

        Office of education   Yes ———— No ————

Office of economic opportunity   Yes _____ No _____

Other _____   Yes _____ No _____

e. Total number of arts events (all arts) from off-campus for which tickets are sold: _____

Total admissions to arts events from off-campus: _____

Total income from arts events from off-campus: _____

Total expenses for arts events from off-campus: _____

f. (1) Do you have a gallery?   Yes _____ No _____

If yes, please continue:

(2) The gallery is operated by:

    (a) the university _____

    (b) the college _____

    (c) the department of visual arts _____

    (d) other _____

(3) The director of the gallery serves as a director:

    (a) full time _____

    (b) ¾ time _____

    (c) ½ time _____

    (d) ¼ time _____

    (e) other _____

(4) The director has a staff of:

    (a) none _____   (d) three _____

    (b) one _____   (e) four _____

    (c) two _____   (f) more _____

g. If the college or the departments offer arts events for which there is a charge, the income is deposited to:

(1) university general funds _____

(2) a university committee controlling student-faculty arts events _____

(3) student body funds _____

(4) the college _____

(5) the department involved _____

(6) other _____

h. The college and/or the departments are provided with funds in the budget over and above any box office returns to produce arts events:

Yes _____ No _____

i. If yes, the budgets for this purpose annually amount to:

    (1) College $_____   (6) Theater $_____

    (2) Architecture $_____   (7) Writing $_____

    (3) Dance $_____   (8) Visual arts $_____

    (4) Film $_____   (9) Other $_____

    (5) Music $_____

j. The following undergraduate scholarships and graduate fellowships, teaching and otherwise, are awarded annually:

	Number of undergraduate scholarships	Total amount in dollars	Number of graduate fellowships	Total amount in dollars
Architecture				
Dance				
Film				
Music				
Theater				
Writing				
Visual arts				
Other				

24. This is highly subjective, of course, but would you express your feelings as to your departments' (faculty) effectiveness in the following:
   a. Contribution of new works in performance and exhibits:
      (1) very effective _____
      (2) moderately   _____
      (3) not enough   _____
      Comments: _____
   b. Development of an increasingly sophisticated laity (audience):
      (1) very effective _____
      (2) moderately   _____
      (3) not enough   _____
      Comments: _____
   c. Exploration of contemporary trends (arts movements):
      (1) very effective _____
      (2) moderately   _____
      (3) not enough   _____
      Comments: _____
   d. Vital, stimulating exploration of the heritage of each of the arts to introduce the seminal forces of the past:
      (1) very effective _____
      (2) moderately   _____
      (3) not enough   _____
      Comments: _____
   e. Seeking new relationship in the arts:
      (1) very effective _____
      (2) moderately   _____
      (3) not enough   _____
      Comments: _____

25. a. Do you maintain a systematic follow-up study of your graduates in each of the arts? Yes _____ No _____

(Should the university include this as a responsibility of the Office of Institutional Research? Yes _____ No _____)

b. Are you satisfied with your contribution to the number of "successful" working artists (in the sense of making significant contributions to the various fields professionally)?

Faculty: Yes _____ No _____

Student: Yes _____ No _____

Comments: _____

26. Do you feel your college is having any appreciable effect on the content and procedures of education in the arts in the schools—kindergarten through twelfth grade—in your state?

Yes _____ No _____

(If yes or no, please offer your analysis of this condition.)

_____

_____

27. a. Do you feel that there is, overall, good rapport (rather than a "generation gap") between faculty and students as to the growth and development of each of the fields of the arts?

Yes _____ No _____

Comment: _____

b. In this regard, is there a growing question of the efficacy of tenure for faculty in the arts in your university?

Yes _____ No _____

Comment: _____

c. Do your faculty have time for "creative research," pursuing their own work in the arts?

Yes _____ No _____

Comment: _____

d. How many faculty (full-time FTE), part-time faculty (bodies and sum of all part-time FTE), and student teaching assistants do you have in each of the arts?

	Number of full-time faculty FTE	Number of part-time faculty (bodies)	Sum of all FTE's	Number of student teaching assistants
Architecture				
Dance				
Film				
Music				
Theater				
Writing				
Visual arts				
Other				
Other				

Comment: _____

28. Do you believe in and have evidence, to your satisfaction, of a growing surge of interest and pursuit of the arts in:
    a. your student majors: Yes _____ No _____
    b. the general student body: Yes _____ No _____
    Comment: _____

29. Do you have any impression, hunch, or hard evidence that educating students will demand more technological equipment or that a trend is toward the simpler, more humanized technologies? For example, synthetic sound vis-à-vis the guitar, mechanized theatres vis-à-vis street theatre, or ecumenical communal arts living groups (Bread-and-Puppet Theatre) vis-à-vis the heavy budget demanding centers (Lincoln Center)?
    a. Technology-oriented _____
    b. Simple, humanized approach _____
    c. Both are required _____
    Comment: _____

30. Please make any further statement and suggestions here. (For example: Have any key aspects of the arts been omitted? What of the above do you consider inconsequential?)
    _____
    _____
    _____
    _____

_____

_____

_____

_____

_____

_____

_____

_____

_____

_____

_____

_____

(Please use back of page.)

Return to: Dr. Jack Morrison, The JDR 3rd Fund, 50 Rockefeller Plaza New York, New York 10020.

Index

This book was set in Vladimir by University Graphics, Inc.
It was printed on acid-free, long-life paper and bound by The
Maple Press Company. The designers were Elliot Epstein and
Edward Butler. The editors were Nancy Tressel and Janine Parson
for McGraw-Hill Book Company and Verne A. Stadtman and Terry
Y. Allen for the Carnegie Commission on Higher Education.
Joe Campanella and William Greenwood supervised the production.